AFRICA TECHNICAL DEPARTMENT SERIES

Technical Paper Series

No. 122 Dessing, *Support for Microenterprises: Lessons for Sub-Saharan Africa*

No. 130 Kiss, editor, *Living with Wildlife: Wildlife Resource Management with Local Participation in Africa*

No. 132 Murphy, Casley, and Curry, *Farmers' Estimations as a Source of Production Data: Methodological Guidelines for Cereals in Africa*

No. 135 Walshe, Grindle, Nell, and Bachmann, *Dairy Development in Sub-Saharan Africa: A Study of Issues and Options*

No. 141 Riverson, Gaviria, and Thriscutt, *Rural Roads in Sub-Saharan Africa: Lessons from World Bank Experience*

No. 142 Kiss and Meerman, *Integrated Pest Management and African Agriculture*

No. 143 Grut, Gray, and Egli, *Forest Pricing and Concession Policies: Managing the High Forests of West and Central Africa*

No. 157 Critchley, Reij, and Seznec, *Water Harvesting for Plant Production*, vol. II: *Case Studies and Conclusions for Sub-Saharan Africa*

No. 161 Riverson and Carapetis, *Intermediate Means of Transport in Sub-Saharan Africa: Its Potential for Improving Rural Travel and Transport*

No. 165 Kellaghan and Greaney, *Using Examinations to Improve Education: A Study in Fourteen African Countries*

No. 179 Speirs and Olsen, *Indigenous Integrated Farming Systems in the Sahel*

No. 181 Mining Unit, Industry and Energy Division, *Strategy for African Mining*

Discussion Paper Series

No. 82 Psacharopoulos, *Why Educational Policies Can Fail: An Overview of Selected African Experiences*

No. 83 Craig, *Comparative African Experiences in Implementing Educational Policies*

No. 84 Kiros, *Implementing Educational Policies in Ethiopia*

No. 85 Eshiwani, *Implementing Educational Policies in Kenya*

No. 86 Galabawa, *Implementing Educational Policies in Tanzania*

No. 87 Thelejani, *Implementing Educational Policies in Lesotho*

No. 88 Magalula, *Implementing Educational Policies in Swaziland*

No. 89 Odaet, *Implementing Educational Policies in Uganda*

No. 90 Achola, *Implementing Educational Policies in Zambia*

No. 91 Maravanyika, *Implementing Educational Policies in Zimbabwe*

No. 101 Russell, Jacobsen, and Stanley, *International Migration and Development in Sub-Saharan Africa*, vol. I: *Overview*

No. 102 Russell, Jacobsen, and Stanley, *International Migration and Development in Sub-Saharan Africa*, vol. II: *Country Analyses*

No. 132 Fuller and Habte, editors, *Adjusting Educational Policies: Conserving Resources while Raising School Quality*

No. 147 Jaeger, *The Effects of Economic Policies on African Agriculture: From Past Harm to Future Hope*

175

World Bank Discussion Papers
Africa Technical Department Series

Resource Management and Pastoral Institution Building in the West African Sahel

Nadarajah Shanmugaratnam,
Trond Vedeld, Anne Mossige, and
Mette Bovin

The World Bank
Washington, D.C.

Manufactured in the United States of America
First printing December 1992

Discussion Papers present results of country analysis or research that is circulated to encourage discussion and comment within the development community. To present these results with the least possible delay, the typescript of this paper has not been prepared in accordance with the procedures appropriate to formal printed texts, and the World Bank accepts no responsibility for errors.

The findings, interpretations, and conclusions expressed in this paper are entirely those of the author(s) and should not be attributed in any manner to the World Bank, to its affiliated organizations, or to members of its Board of Executive Directors or the countries they represent. The World Bank does not guarantee the accuracy of the data included in this publication and accepts no responsibility whatsoever for any consequence of their use. Any maps that accompany the text have been prepared solely for the convenience of readers; the designations and presentation of material in them do not imply the expression of any opinion whatsoever on the part of the World Bank, its affiliates, or its Board or member countries concerning the legal status of any country, territory, city, or area or of the authorities thereof or concerning the delimitation of its boundaries or its national affiliation.

The complete backlist of publications from the World Bank is shown in the annual *Index of Publications,* which contains an alphabetical title list (with full ordering information) and indexes of subjects, authors, and countries and regions. The latest edition is available free of charge from the Distribution Unit, Office of the Publisher, Department F, The World Bank, 1818 H Street, N.W., Washington, D.C. 20433, U.S.A., or from Publications, The World Bank, 66, avenue d'Iéna, 75116 Paris, France.

ISSN: 0259-210X

At the Norwegian Center for International Agricultural Development (NORAGRIC), at the Agricultural University of Norway Nadarajah Shanmugaratnam is senior resource and institutional economist; Trond Vedeld is an environmental planning research fellow; and Anne Mossige a natural resource management researcher. Mette Bovin is a freelance sociologist consultant.

Library of Congress Cataloging-in-Publication Data

Resource management and pastoral institution building in the West
African Sahel / Nadarajah Shanmugaratnam ... [et al.].
p. cm. — (World Bank discussion papers, ISSN 0259-210X ;
175. Africa Technical Department series)
Includes bibliographical references.
ISBN 0-8213-2215-X
1. Range management—Sahel. 2. Pastoral systems—Sahel.
3. Livestock—Sahel. I. Shanmugaratnam, N. II. Series: World Bank
discussion papers ; 175. III. Series: World Bank discussion papers.
Africa Technical Department series.
SF85.4.S15R47 1992
333.74'0966—dc20 92-29976
CIP

Foreword

This discussion paper presents the results of a study on pastoral institution building and resource management in the West African Sahel. The study was part of a program of research into the future directions of livestock production, agricultural development, and resource management in Sub-Saharan Africa, carried out by the Agricultural Division of the World Bank's Africa Technical Department.

The Norwegian Ministry of Foreign Affairs provided funds for the study, which was conducted by the Norwegian Center for International Agricultural Development (NORAGRIC), Agricultural University of Norway.

The sustainability of traditional pastoralism, the degradation of rangelands, and the loss of traditional grazing lands to cultivation are matters of major concern not only to pastoralists and their governments, but also to the international community at large.

The formation and empowerment of pastoral associations, which would enable local communities to assume responsibility for, and play an active role in, the management of natural resources as well as in the provision of basic services, is now generally accepted as the only worthwhile approach to one of the world's most difficult and complex social and environmental problems.

The study describes the experiences and lessons that have emerged from the implementation of on-going projects, assisted by the World Bank, designed to develop pastoral associations in Mali, Mauritania, Niger, and Senegal.

The findings indicate that the formation and operation of pastoral associations must still be regarded as a pilot development activity, although valuable lessons and recommendations can be deduced, even at this early stage. The challenge now is to incorporate these lessons and recommendations in the design of future projects that aim to establish viable sustainable pastoral institutions and resource management activities.

Pierre Landell-Mills
Acting Director
Technical Department
Africa Region
World Bank

Acknowledgments

This study was undertaken under the auspices of the World Bank. It was initiated and managed by Poul Sihm, Senior Livestock Specialist in the Bank's African Technical Department. Funding for the study was provided by the Norwegian Ministry of Foreign Affairs, and it was conducted by the Norwegian Centre for International Agricultural Development (NORAGRIC), Agricultural University of Norway.

The authors would like to acknowledge the assistance and support provided by project staff and other local experts during field visits. Special thanks are due to Sulmana Cisse (Mali); Brahim Fall Lemine and Pierre Bonte (Mauritania); Amadou Wahabou Thioune (Senegal); Akilou Habou and Patrick Paris (Niger); and pastoral leaders and members of pastoral associations.

The report is based on a review of project documents, recent publications, and field studies. Valuable advice and comments were given by staff of the Agricultural and Environmental Divisions of the World Bank's Africa Technical Department and other Bank staff in the Africa Region. Many useful comments on an earlier draft were made by Roy Behnke (Overseas Development Institute, London); Anders Hjort af Ornas (Scandinavian Institute of African Studies, Uppsala); F. Riveros (FAO, Rome); J. Swift (Institute of Development Studies, University of Sussex); E. P. Cunningham (FAO); and A. E. Sidahmed (FAO). The photographs were taken by Mette Bovin.

We also wish to express our thanks to Michael Walshe, Paula Strawhecker, Leo Demesmaker, and Christina Dhanaraj for their input into the final stages of the study, and to Muriel Prah who handled the desktop publishing.

Contents

Pastoral association's cattle vaccination crush in the Sahel

Abbreviations

AFTAG	Africa Technical Agriculture Division
BIE	Bureau d'Intrants d'Elevage, Mauritania
BNDA	Banque Nationale de Développement d'Agricole, Mali
CCCE	Caisse Centrale de Coopération Economique, France
CP	Centre Pastoral, Niger
CSE	Centre Suivi Ecologique, Dakar
GIE	Groupement d'Intérêt Economique, Senegal
GMP	Groupement Mutualiste Pastoral, Niger
GVC	Groupement à Vocation Coopérative, Niger
MC	Management Committee, Senegal
NGO	Nongovernmental organization
NORAGRIC	Norwegian Centre for International Agricultural Development
NRM	Natural resources management
ODEM	Opération de Développement de l'Elevage dans la Région de Mopti
ODI	Overseas Development Institute
ORM	Opération Riz de Mopti
P 17	Grazing area in Mali (Boni)
PA	Pastoral association, Mali/Mauritania
PCR	Project Completion Report
PCDA	Pastoral Community Development Officer
PDESO	Projet de Développement de l'Elevage au Sénégal Oriental
PENCE	Projet de Développement de l'Elevage au Niger Centre-Est
PICOGERNA	Programme Integré de Conservation et de Gestion des Ressources Naturelles, Sénégal
PO	Pastoral organization
PU	Pastoral unit (geographical unit)
RC	Rural council
SODEFITEX	Société pour le Développement des Fibres Textiles (Cotton Development Agency)
SOMECOB	Société Mauritanienne d'Elevage et de Commercialisation du Bétail
TA	Technical assistance
TLU	Tropical Livestock Unit
WB	World Bank
WFP	World Food Programme
WID	Women in Development

1. Pastoralism in Context

There are 20 to 25 million pastoralists in the drylands of Africa. In many parts of Sub-Saharan Africa, pastoralists exploit the low opportunity cost of natural fodder on lands which are not suited for sustainable agricultural production. In some areas, pastoralism coexists and competes with arable farming. In others, pastoralism is a component of a variety of mixed systems of agro-pastoralism and agro-sylvo-pastoralism.

In recent years pastoralism has been caught in a protracted crisis that has its most dramatic manifestations in frequent famines and the phenomenon of environmental refugees. The politico-military dimensions of the crisis are evident in the internal wars in Africa in which pastoralists are often the major victims.

Competition from agriculture, herd dispossession, wars, drought, and population growth have undermined traditional pastoral institutions and contributed to mass displacement of pastoralists. Most governments and international donors not only assign higher priority to agriculture than to pastoralism, but often do so at the expense of the interests of millions of pastoralists. As a production system and a way of life, pastoralism appears to be fighting a losing battle.

However, there are signs of a new consensus on the importance and development potential of pastoralism. There is also a growing awareness of the social cost of development strategies that exclude pastoralists in the Sahelian countries. Pastoralists contribute to the national economy through the production of milk, meat, leather, wool, animals for traction, and manure for agriculture, and to foreign exchange earnings through the export of livestock and livestock products. They have a key role to play in the rehabilitation and sustainable management of the fragile ecosystems of the Sahel. Political stabilization and democratization, and the reconstruction of the economies of the Sahelian countries overwhelmed by war and famine cannot be accomplished without the participation of the pastoral, agro-pastoral and agro-sylvo-pastoral producers. These considerations have compelled governments and development aid agencies to review their positions on pastoralism.

A manifestation of this new concern is pastoral institution building for sustainable natural resource management and rural development. Institution building is a means to equip pastoralists to overcome the constraints to pastoral development in the Sahel today. Prospects for dramatic increases in range productivity are limited for technological as well as economic reasons; so are prospects for expansion into new areas. Meanwhile, conversion of the best pastoral lands into agricultural lands continues, together with range degradation including loss of trees, causing decline in the resource base for pure pastoralism in many parts of the Sahel.

Today unprecedented numbers of pastoralists and livestock must subsist on an ever-contracting land base, often further reduced by the closure of national borders between some countries. Another important development is the voluntary and involuntary settling of pastoralists. There has been a tendency toward voluntary settling since the drought of 1972-73, increasing after subsequent droughts, and often accompanied by a transition from pure pastoralism to agro-pastoralism in which agriculture is subsistence-oriented and highly risky. The consequences of drought and dispossession have also driven many pastoralists to become waged-herders and manual workers, and into towns where they join the unemployed and the slum dwellers.

The future of pastoralism depends on the ecological restoration and sustainable utilization of the available rangelands, on the improvement of livestock productivity, and the resolution of resource conflicts in ways that facilitate the integration of pastoralism, agriculture, and sylviculture in areas suitable for their coexistence.

These challenges require institutional innovations to deal with the new dimensions of old problems such as land and water rights and herd regeneration after drought. Moreover, the pastoralists find themselves in a world which demands new skills. They have to be able to communicate with the government in the official language, comprehend new laws governing their traditional resources, practice some form of accounting and book-keeping to manage their local institutions, deal with political organizations, struggle for better marketing facilities and more reasonable terms of trade, and relate to rural banks and other sources of credit.

A great need for pastoral institutions is felt by the pastoralists themselves who have learned that they must come to terms with the state for economic and well as political reasons.

Background to the Study

The present study reviews experiences in the formation of pastoral institutions in government-sponsored development projects assisted by the World Bank in Mali, Mauritania, Niger, and Senegal, with the particular objective of assessing their potential as custodians of natural resources and participants in sustainable resource management.

In each case, the program for pastoral organization and training was one component of a multi-component development project with a broader focus on "livestock" or "agriculture".

This report is based on project documents, recent literature on issues pertaining to pastoralism and natural resources management in the Sahel, and thirty person-weeks of fieldwork in the countries concerned. During the fieldwork, national experts contributed significantly to the study.

A major constraint to the study was the lack of basic data on the formation and performance of pastoral organizations (POs) in any of the four projects. None of the projects had a proper monitoring and evaluation system for the PO component. Efforts to collect quantitative data on POs when they were visited in the course of fieldwork were limited by the absence of records and lack of time.

Regarding terms, Sandford (1983), is followed in defining "pastoralists" as people who derive most of their income or sustenance from keeping domestic livestock in conditions where most of the feed eaten by their livestock is natural forage, not cultivated fodders and pastures. In its broadest sense "pastoralism" refers to the way of life of pastoralists, their socio-economic institutions and land-use systems. The definition adopted here covers "pure" pastoralism, and other mixed forms in which the pastoral component is dominant, for example agro-pastoralism and agro-sylvo-pastoralism.

"Pastoral organizations" (POs) is used as a generic term to cover all types of institutional arrangements that regulate individual and collective actions by pastoralists to safeguard and promote their economic, social, cultural, and political interests. The functions of POs vary over a wide range. Sandford (1981) classifies them into six groups: land tenure, resource management, provision of services, communication of information, external relations, and the building and maintenance of community cohesion and morale. A pastoral organization may be responsible for one or more of these functions.

This study is mainly concerned with state-sponsored POs in projects assisted by the World Bank. These POs may be called by different names in the different countries. In Senegal, for example, they are Groupement d'Intérêt Economique (GIE); in Niger, Groupement Mutualiste Pastoral (GMP) and Groupement à Vocation

Coopérative (GVC), and in Mali and Mauritania, Associations Pastorales (AP). Most of the these POs are legally constituted bodies recognized by the government. They are dependent on the state for technical services, supplies, and financial resources. Governments may promote certain types of POs for political and economic reasons; for example, to incorporate pastoral communities more effectively into the national political and administrative systems, or to exercise control over land resources and their utilization.

"Natural resources management" (NRM) covers all aspects of water and rangeland management, including the operation of water and land rights, water point management, range management such as grazing schemes, bushfire control, sand dune stabilization, tree protection and planting, as well as resolution of resource-use conflict, and animal husbandry related to grazing management, including transhumance, adjustment of stocking rates, and change in species composition.

Pastoral Organizations as Natural Resource Managers

As water resources and dry season grazing diminish, their sustained utilization requires revised regulatory arrangements. Simultaneously, traditional resource management systems are disintegrating and traditional survival strategies becoming obsolete, pointing to the need for new forms of community-based natural resource management.

The Sahelian states do not have any effective instruments to enforce property rights and manage range and water resources at the local level. Community-based NRM systems with state assistance in the form of enforcement of property rights seem to be the most feasible option. POs can become instruments of decentralization and local development. They can participate in the privatization of services like distribution of veterinary drugs and human provisions. However, there may be differences between the pastoralists, the government, and donors in perceptions of the institutional needs.

It has become clear to governments and donors that both pastoralism and agriculture in the Sahel have become more vulnerable to environmental stress. NRM is an explicitly recognized policy issue. However, policies are not always guided by considerations of sustainable resource management alone. There are political forces and ethnic conflicts at work which may push NRM down to a lower priority. As a result, governments and livestock projects may fail to fully utilize the favorable conditions for pastoral institution building. There can also be differences between a government and a donor in the specifics of project planning and implementation. For instance, the World Bank has emphasized the importance of local capacity-building as an aspect of creating an enabling environment for rural development. A recipient government may accept this in principle but may not be able to achieve it in a project for political or logistical reasons.

An Enabling Environment

The main elements of **an enabling environment for POs** would include the following:

- legal recognition of POs to function as autonomous bodies on matters relating to NRM, and defensible land and water rights,
- basic infrastructure and services such as health and education,
- competent leadership,
- animal health services,
- NRM training facilities,
- means of raising the economic self-reliance of POs through income-generating activities,
- representation of the different social strata and ethnic groups of the pastoral population in the POs,
- marketing outlets
- access to NRM technology and,
- efficient channels of communication between POs and between POs and the project

and local and central governments.

Satisfaction of these requirements presupposes government commitment and requires effective policy action by all four of the players involved: the central government, the local government, the project, and the nascent PO.

The extent to which these elements were already in place, or were put into place as the pastoral organization structures were being formed, will be seen in the country reviews.

A well in the Mauritanian Sahel

2. Measurements of Success

Livestock projects in Sub-Saharan Africa funded by the World Bank and other international agencies have in the past often performed far below expectations (Sandford 1981, World Bank 1988). Critics have pointed out that the causes of failure lay in the narrow technical approaches to development which neglected the social, cultural and ecological particularities of pastoral production. While the first generation of projects assisted by the World Bank such as the Kenyan Group Ranches, launched in the 1960s, emphasized ranching of various forms inspired by African and Western commercial ranching experience in livestock development, the second generation projects put emphasis on rangeland development. The focus was on animals and rangeland, rather than on herders and people.

These approaches often failed to produce satisfactory results from a development point of view. A basic shortcoming was their inability to take into account the complexities, and the development potentials and constraints of traditional pastoral organizations. Little or no attention was paid to institution building at local and intermediary level to mobilize and strengthen capacities to manage pastoral resources and development. This meant that some of the most fundamental problems of pastoral development were defined out of the projects' concern.

The failures of the past interventions have provoked some new thinking in the World Bank and the evolution of new approaches to pastoral development based on broader premises such as sustainable NRM, policy and institutional reforms, local institution building, and integrated approaches to agro-sylvo-pastoral development backed by system studies and environmental monitoring. The guiding philosophy as regards institution building is to allow solutions to evolve instead of imposing them (Lewis 1989). In the recent policy discussions in the World Bank, there is an explicit recognition of the site-specificity of pastoral problems in the drylands and the need to adopt a longer time perspective on pastoral development (Sihm 1989, Lewis 1989).

These changes are reflected to some degree in the design profile of the projects under review. The budget allocations for PO development and training are, however, still low compared to the allocations for other program components. As in the past, veterinary health, water, and rangeland development remain the dominant components of the current projects in terms of financial allocations. The rather significant changes in the conceptualization of the problems and approaches to pastoral development are not fully reflected in the budgets of the project. A significant change is the increased budget allocations for agriculture, crop-livestock integration and agro-pastoralism.

Key Factors

Since the initiative for PO formation in the projects under review came from above, the progress and success of the institution building process would depend on how quickly and effectively this initiative from above could be turned into a stimulus for a grassroots participatory process. This depended largely on the identification of "rallying points" or key functions around which the POs should be established. The rallying points have to be clearly identified through dialogues with the intended beneficiaries. Pastoralists evaluate NRM as a means to specific ends which determine the overall socio-economic security of households and groups, and in terms of their own priorities based on experience. Adequate knowledge of these priorities is essential to work out strategies of mobilization and to achieve participation. For example, while small cohesive groups can more efficiently manage water points, management of viable units of rangeland requires larger groups formed by combining several small cohesive groups. This is a major task in PO formation and may demand considerable time and professional resources.

Another important point is the concept of membership in a PO. Some criteria are necessary to distinguish a PO member from a non-member within a local group. An individual pastoralist may not be inclined to join a PO if, in his perception, membership involves only obligations in terms of time, money, or responsibility, and no tangible short- or long-term benefits; for example, if access to water, pasture, and animal health services is not affected by individual membership, the incentive to be a free rider may be strong.

With these considerations in mind, several key factors, from the national to the local levels, can be identified, which can be helpful in evaluating progress in pastoral institution building. These factors are directly connected with the tasks of creating an enabling environment for POs. Several basic conditions have to be satisfied at the central government policy level to create an enabling environment for POs at the local level. These include:

• The political will and policy commitment to empower pastoralists, and support pastoral institution building, demonstrated through tenurial reform granting defensible land and water rights to pastoralists,

- enforcement of effective property rights,

- decentralization of development decisionmaking.

• Appropriate livestock price, taxation, and marketing policies to encourage livestock development through pastoralism

• National literacy, and human, and animal health programs for pastoral areas

• Public investment in rural infrastructure.

• Support for POs' participation in privatization of animal services and distribution of provisions.

• Coordination of policies and operations at field level, mechanisms for intersectoral planning and conflict resolution.

• Respect for ethno-cultural identities of pastoralists.

At project level, the following factors can be identified:

• The project's commitment to and financial allocation for pastoral institution building

• The models of POs - the concepts, basic unit, organizational aggregation and hierarchy

• Professional competence of the project implementing agency,

• Participation of women on project staff

• Communication and cooperation between the project and the government's administrative bodies

At the PO level, a major consideration in forming the type of PO which will succeed is the type of pastoralism it serves: namely nomadic, transhumant, or sedentary; pure pastoralism or agro-pastoralism. The PO formation process should be seen in its specific socio-cultural setting with prevailing social structures and traditional institutions. A key factor is the basis of mobilization and group formation, and the size of the local group and its spatial spread. The agro-ecological and climatic conditions in which transhumance normally takes place are also important determinants, for example, whether the pastoral areas are mainly in arid/semi-arid or sub-humid zones. The legal status of the PO is important too, particularly when dealing with government bodies, NGOs, and lending institutions. The other key factors for assessment are:

- Food security
- Resource security and management
  - Water security
  - Land security
  - Natural resource management
- Herd ownership
- Services
  - Credit
  - Animal health
  - Human health
  - Marketing
  - Literacy
  - Management training
- Mobilization and participation of men and women
- Leadership quality
  - Capacity to mobilize the people
  - Capacity to deal with project and government authorities
  - Technical know-how
    - NRM
    - Book-keeping and accounting
- Economic viability of the PO
- Degree of dependence/self sufficiency

Significance of the Key Factors

These key factors will determine the viability of the pastoral organizations, and provide a framework for analysis of their progress which is described in Chapter 3. Their special importance to pastoralists is now summarized.

Food security

Food security, on which life depends, is uppermost in the minds of pastoralists. In explaining the utmost importance of food security, Sahelian pastoralists refer to their sufferings during and after the droughts of 1972-74 and 1983-84 when traditional mechanisms of survival broke down. They also say that the most important reason for selling animals is to buy cereals, tea and sugar. A pastoral household's food security is determined by its ability to command the goods and services needed to satisfy the nutritional needs of its members. In times of drought and food crisis the terms of trade turn unfavorable to pastoralists. In fact, the seasonal movements of livestock-cereal terms of trade are most unfavorable to herders when their dependence on purchased grains is highest. Official price policies, poor infrastructure and lack of organizations to promote pastoralists' interests compound the effects of environmental factors.

POs can strengthen food security by improving the marketing facilities for livestock and by procuring and distributing food and other essentials through cereal banks and cooperative shops. These can be run on revolving funds which are often initially supplied partly or fully by external donors. The size of the fund and its rate of expansion are useful indicators of organizational development. POs can also operate distress loan schemes, organize dry season animal feed supply in the form of fodder banks, and arrange advance stocking of supplementary feeding stuff by purchasing it when prices are low.

Water security

Water security covers water availability, water rights, and water management. The first means the number and spatial distribution of water points which may be temporary (seasonal ponds and streams) or permanent (wells, boreholes, and perennial rivers and ponds). Water rights determine access which depends on ownership: water points may be owned privately, communally, or by the state (public wells). The crucial factor is the existing regulations for water use by herders and the system of management of water points. When public wells are open to all without any controls, as is often the case, rangeland around them becomes open access too, causing range degradation. Any herder can claim a right to water from a public well and as a result also gain access to the grazing land around. The solution is to convert public wells into collective assets of POs.

Drawing water from wells and boreholes (maintaining them) involves costs in labor, draft animals, materials, pumps, and fuel. On the other hand control of wells and boreholes provides a good opportunity to generate revenue for the PO by charging the herders for the water supplied to their herds. Control of waterpoints provides opportunities to indirectly control access to the rangelands around them.

Land security

All pastoralists—sedentary, transhumant or nomadic—have their own sense of territorial identities. There has been a trend of voluntary settlement among pastoralists in the Sahel in the past two decades. Agro-pastoralists who are among the most sedentary identify themselves with certain territories. Transhumants, who may also practice seasonal agriculture, have their "base areas" where the families stay while the younger men or hired herders transhume with the herds. Nomadic pastoralists have their traditional patterns of mobility and seasonal pastures. The nature of land and water rights demanded by these different types of pastoralists varies. Equally important are well established principles of reciprocity between different groups, and informally recognized priority rights of access to water and pastures. Even with a group that identifies itself with a certain territory, there is no notion of rigidly fixed physical boundaries. The frontiers are variable according to the amount and distribution of rainfall. Even under the most sedentary conditions the spatial unit is a dynamic category.

A legal concept of land rights and spatial demarcation should recognize the principle of reciprocity between resource users identifying themselves with different territories and the dynamic character of the physical limits of such territories. It should also accommodate the interdependence between agricultural, agro-pastoral, and pure pastoral zones. It should recognize that there are potential resource-use conflicts between pastoralism and agricultural production, and that such conflicts have increased in frequency and scale.

Spatial demarcation with secure, defensible usufruct rights is a basic condition for the sustainable management of the rangeland with its pastures and trees. Overgrazing and desertification in the Sahel have become so controversial it is not easy to choose a side. Apparently, Sahelian rangelands have greater resilience than assumed by the "desertification" school. Their carrying capacity is not constant but varies according to the amount and distribution of rainfall. Pastoralists adopt opportunistic strategies to adapt to such fluctuations in pasture availability. In times of abundance of pasture, they strive to build their herds as fast as they can to exploit the opportunity for conversion of green biomass into milk and meat. This strategy is also helpful in ensuring that at least a few animals survive a drought that may follow. Some have argued that this is the best way to utilize the range in the Sahel (Behnke and Scoones 1990). It should suffice to state that overgrazing and land degradation do exist as localized phenomena in certain areas and are recognized by the pastoralists themselves. Loss of trees has reached alarming proportions in many areas, and along with overgrazing has promoted movements of sand dunes. Rangelands are also damaged by accidental bushfires which seem to outnumber those deliberately created. These factors make rangeland management an important priority for POs.

Herd ownership

The main purpose of herd keeping by pastoralists is milk with meat production secondary. They sell livestock to meet their cash needs. These have been increasing over the years. Milk productivity influences pastoralists' decisions about herd size. Herd size and species composition (the proportion of cattle, small ruminants, camels) are also determined by the ecological conditions, anticipation of droughts in terms of insurance against risk, and the "banking" role of livestock as a source of economic return, a growing stock of capital, and as an asset that can be converted into cash. The growth of absentee herd ownership is also related to the "banking" role of livestock in the absence of more attractive investment opportunities for traders, civil servants, and farmers.

Credit

Institutional credit has remained inaccessible to the vast majority of pastoralists in Africa because of their inability to provide legally valid security. The removal of this disability requires governmental action and the innovation of credit schemes that can be operated among pastoralists. A crucial need for credit is to regenerate herds at the individual household level, but a pastoralist without animals has practically nothing to offer as security. The scale of dispossession of herders is so high in the Sahel, that a radical policy intervention is needed to work out and implement mechanisms to redistribute the existing animal populations. Such a radical reform, when coupled with a land and water tenurial reform, can be a powerful rallying point to mobilize herders to organize themselves into POs for sustainable resource management. POs can step in and provide a collective guarantee for their members for a herd regeneration credit scheme in kind.

Veterinary services

The overall performance of the veterinary services in the project area may be an indicator of the project's achievement in animal health. The present concern, however, is the extent of participation of the POs in managing basic veterinary facilities and the efficiency of the supply of veterinary services and drugs, which can be assessed by the number of pastoralists trained as veterinary workers, the work they carry out, and the coverage and costs of veterinary services including drugs to herders. Are POs running their own pharmacies and if so, how efficient are they compared to other suppliers? Pharmacy operation by a PO would require revolving funds and management skills and financial discipline.

Marketing

POs can play a role in improving the local marketing channels provided that price policies are not unfavorable and basic transport and communication facilities exist. Lack of infrastructure has been a major barrier to commercialization of the livestock sector in the Sahel. Private traders may appear to be efficient intermediaries in livestock marketing, but the more important question is the terms of trade between livestock and grain producers. In times of crisis pastoralists are forced to resort to distress sale. Given the poor, sometimes nonexistent, communication infrastructure and the seasonality and risks affecting both livestock and crop production, generalized free markets cannot operate in many areas. Any role in marketing can be considered only where such constraints do not exist.

Economic self-sufficiency

The viability of a PO can be assessed by its ability to generate its own revenues through charges for services, membership fees, taxes, and the planned expansion of revolving funds. A reasonable idea of progress in economic viability can be formed by relating the financial status of a PO to the period of its existence. Quality of leadership, literacy levels of the members, the extent of membership mobilization and active participation, financial management skills, creditworthiness of the PO, and management training are among the most important determinants. For tax collection to raise economic viability, the authority would have to be delegated by the government.

Literacy

Literacy is a prerequisite for participation in the management of POs and for the acquisition of new skills like book-keeping and accounting, resource planning, legal knowledge, correspondence in the official language, and basic medical knowledge. Literacy provides self-confidence in dealing with the government and the outside world. Traditional leaders are generally not literate and are unable to fulfil the new roles demanded of them. They can be successfully challenged and replaced by the more literate who are able to satisfy the new leadership demands. It is essential to create as large a pool as possible of literate members of both sexes at the local level so that leadership is not monopolized by a tiny minority of literate males. The level of literacy in the project area and whether or not it is covered by the national literacy programs are important considerations. A link between the project's program and the national elementary educational system is essential to ensure the continuity of the literacy campaign. Though a prerequisite, literacy alone is not a sufficient motivating factor for an individual pastoralist to become involved in the affairs of a PO.

Table 1. Cost Allocations to Components of Selected Livestock Development Projects
(million US dollars and percent)

	Mali				*Mauritania*				*Niger*		*Senegal*			
	I		*II*		*I*		*II*				*I*		*II*	
	1975-84		*1986-92*		*1971-79*		*1987-92*		*1979-89*		*1976-80*		*1983-88*	
	$	%	$	%	$	%	$	%	$	%	$	%	$	%
Pastoral organization and training[a]	0.1	1	1.4	3	-	-	2.4	13	-	-	0.2	2	-	-
Livestock services														
Range management	1.5	9	0.4	1	0.6	10	1.6	8	-	-	4.4[e]	34	2.9[d]	(6)
Water development	3.4	20	4.8	12	3.1	52	1.6	(8)	-	-	4.7	35[d]	2.9	(6)
Animal health and extension	3.2	18	2.0	5	1.3	22	2.3	12	0.9	6	1.4	11	2.9	6
Credit[b]	-	-	0.3	1	-	-	-	-	0.5	3	0.4	3	-	-
Infrastructure (roads/distr. systems)	-	-	-	-	-	-	1.7	9	2.5	17	-	-	-	-
Research & Studies & M & E[c]	1.0	6	3.6	9	-	-	2.0	11	-	-	-	-	-	-
Marketing & Abattoir	0.7	4	0.2	1	-	-	1.0	5	-	-	-	-	-	-
Project management	2.4	13	6.9	16	-	-	1.9	10	2.9	19	1.9	15	-	-
Agricultural development	-	-	13.4	32	-	-	-	-	5.3	35	-	-	34.0	71
Contingencies	5.1	29	8.7	20	1.0	16	6.0	32	2.9	20	-	-	10.8	23
Total	17.4	100	41.7	100	6.0	100	18.9	100	15.0	100	13.0	100	47.7	100

Note: The allocation of costs to the individual project components is not completely consistent in the data sources. The project component categories in the table are therefore not fully comparable between the projects. For example, the cost of a particular range management activity may be allocated to 'range management' in one project and to 'extension' in another. The table should therefore be interpreted with some caution.

a. The project component includes training and direct support to the PO formation process. Some costs for training are, however, allocated to 'extension' or 'project management', for example, in Senegal and Niger.

b. Costs for 'credit' are not always separated from costs allocated to other components, for example, in Mauritania.

c. The component includes livestock research, system studies, project start-up costs, and monitoring and evaluation.

d. The brackets indicate that it has not been possible to separate the costs of this component from those allocated to another component. The costs of this component are included in the total allocated to the other component.

e. Includes US$2.3 mill. for firebreaks.

Source: World Bank data

Box 1. Basic Information about the Projects and their Progress

	Mali	*Mauritania*	*Niger*	*Senegal*
Project period: Phase I	1975-79	1971-79	1979-84(89)	1976-80
Phase II	1986-92	1987-92(95)		1983-88(90)
Project area (sq. km)	95,000	130,000	75,000	14,000
Population of project area	100,000	180,000	70-80,000	70,000
No. of POs approved	35 PA	14 PA	147GMP/9GVC/6CP	59 PU/60 GIE
Years under operation (average)	5 yrs	1-2 yrs	4-5 yrs	10 yrs/5 yrs
Area per PO (sq. km)	not available	2,500	not available	240
Population per PO	not available	14,000	GMP:200/GVC:1500	1,200
Total membership as percentage of potential	not available	not available	25%	50%
Direct allocation for PO formation as percentage of total project budget (approx.)	less than 5%	about 10%	less than 5%	about 10%
Project staff for PO formation				
Sociologists	2	1	2	1
Community development officers	none	5 (14 programmed)	6	10 (literacy)
Women officers	1	1	none	1
Food security				
Milk and meat production schemes	a few	a few	a few	several
Distress loan for food security	none	none	none	none
Cereal bank/ Coop.shop	a few	none	a few	none
Water security and management				
Water availability	satisfactory	inadequate	inadeq./satis.	inadeq./satis.
Water rights (PO wells)	unresolved	unresolved	partly resolved	unresolved
Water management committees	a few	not started	for all PO wells	a few for boreholes only

Box 1. (continued)

	Mali	*Mauritania*	*Niger*	*Senegal*
Land security and management				
Spatial delineation	incomplete	done	incomplete	done
Land rights	unresolved	unresolved (process started)	unresolved	resolved
Project grazing scheme	not started	not started	not started	in operation
Range management				
Awareness	high	high	high	high
Pasture management	inadequate	inadequate	inadequate	rel. satisfac.
Firebreak maintenance	inadequate	inadequate	no (training)	inadequate
Tree protection	yes (inadeq.)	yes (inadeq.)	no (training)	yes (inadeq.)
Tree planting	no	no	no	yes (inadeq.)
Dune stabilization	no	some	some by project	n.a
Herd ownership				
Absentee ownership	high (80%?)	high (40%?)	medium/high?	low?
Paid herding	high?	high?	medium/high?	low?
Reconstitution credit	no	no	yes (inadeq.)	no
Credit services				
Availability	low	low	low	low
Management	not available	only recently started	rel. high repayment in kind	60-90% repayment
Animal health services				
AH service officers	212	not available	34	21
PO auxiliaries	none	14 (others under training)	81	140
Marketing services	inadequate	inadequate	inadequate	inadequate
Literacy program				
Project component	yes (inadeq.)	nil (not programmed)	yes (inadeq.)	yes (10% of total pop.)
National program	inadequate	inadequate	nil	inadequate

Box 1. (continued)

	Mali	*Mauritania*	*Niger*	*Senegal*
Human health				
Project component	yes (inadeq.)	nil (not programmed)	yes (inadeq.)	nil (not programmed)
National program	inadequate	inadequate	nil	inadequate
Management training	nil	programmed	inadequate	inadequate
Women's participation	nil	nil	nil	nil
Leadership skills				
Literacy	low	medium	low	low
NRM	low	medium	medium	medium/high
Economic management	low	low	low	low/medium
Conflict resolution	low	medium	low/medium	medium
Promotion of pastoral interests	weak	strong	weak/medium	medium
Economic viability				
Revenue generation	low	low	low	low
External dependence	high	high	high	high

n.a: not applicable
not available: Data not available
PA: Pastoral Association
PU: Pastoral Unit (geographical unit)
GIE: Groupement d'Interét Economique
GMP: Groupement Mutualiste Pastoral
GVC: Groupement à Vocation Coopérative
CP: Centre Pastoral

Source: World Bank data

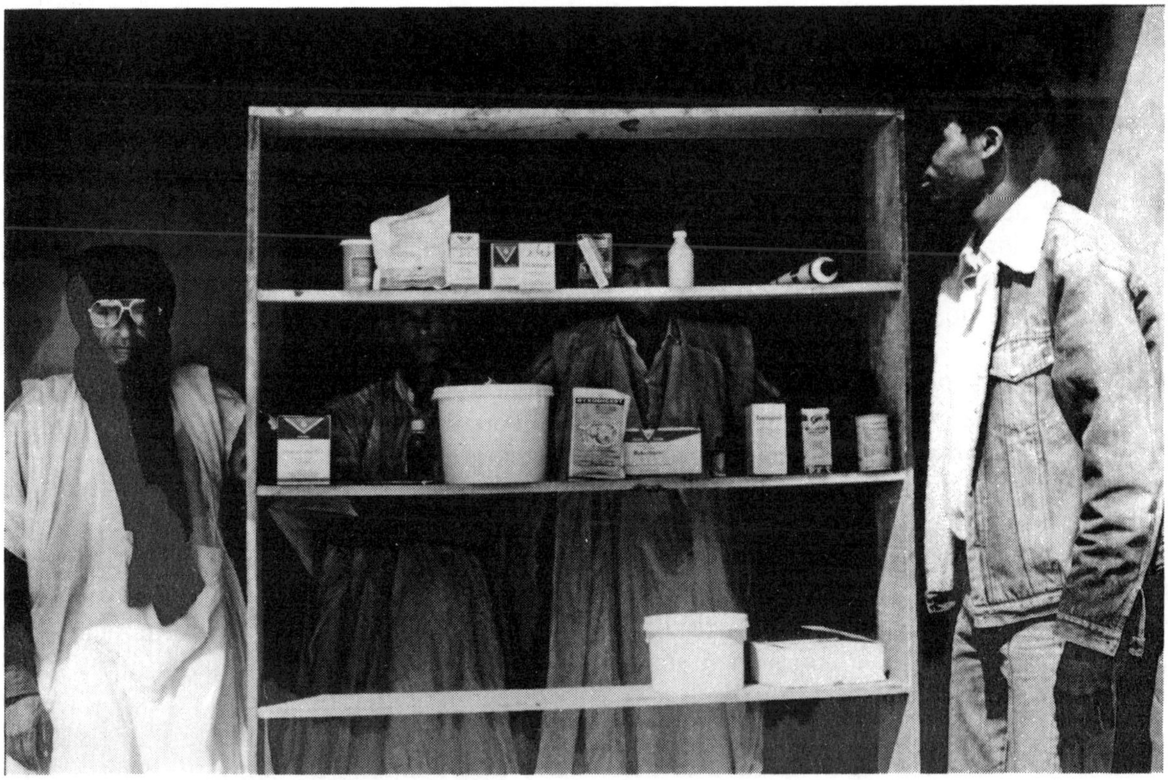

A pastoral association's veterinary pharmacy in Mauritania

3. *Experiences in Pastoral Institution Building*

This chapter describes the experiences in pastoral organization building in the four countries under study, generally highlighting the key factors set out in the analytical framework in Chapter 2.

The requirements of pastoral organization formation and natural resource management share many common elements in the four countries. However, the countries differ in the specifics of their approaches according to the role assumed by the government, the relative importance attached to PO development, the quality of the project management and many other factors.

Box 1 summarizes basic information about the projects and their performance.

Table 1 shows the cost allocations to pastoral organization and training in relation to the other components of the development projects, both in terms of US dollars and percent of total budget.

Mali

At the request of the Government of Mali, the World Bank has been assisting livestock development in the Mopti area since 1975. Among the main objectives of the Mali Livestock Project (1975-84) were rebuilding herds after the 1972-73 drought and rationalizing range and water use. ODEM was the government body established in 1975 under the Ministry of Livestock to implement the project. The second phase of the project was named the Mopti Area Development Project (1985-91) and had both livestock and agricultural components. One of its aims was integration of crop and livestock production. The crop production component was confined to rice monoculture in the Niger delta, with a separate body, ORM (Opération Riz Mopti), set up under the Ministry of Agriculture to implement it.

The overall project was intended to benefit about 100,000 pastoral families in an area of 95,000 square kilometers. The target populations are mainly Peul (Fulani) and Tuareg (Tamachek). Tuaregs predominantly inhabit the northern parts of the project area and their herds have a higher proportion of small ruminants than those of the Peuls. Camels are found almost exclusively in the north. Peuls live mostly in the southern areas. In the past two decades, the traditional structures and institutions have been coming under growing pressures due to the market economy, droughts, dispossession and status-leveling, and dramatic changes in herd ownership patterns.

Large numbers of Peul and Tuareg herders have been dispossessed of their cattle by droughts and by sale to absentee herd owners who are traders, civil servants and farmers. Researchers and others familiar with the project area believe that as much as 80 percent of the herds may belong to absentee owners, although there are no data to support this figure. Since the 1972-73 drought there has been a growing trend of settlement around permanent water points among the traditionally nomadic Tuaregs, accompanied by agriculture of a highly subsistence nature. Many Tuareg families who became destitute because of drought and dispossession, saw their Bella slaves leave for the delta and other parts of the country to become waged workers and cultivators. Many Tuaregs have become waged workers too. The Tuaregs, who traditionally subsisted mainly on milk and meat, have become grain consumers. Many of the former slaves in the Peul hierarchy, the Rimaibe, are today enterprising agriculturalists in the delta and among the growing number of absentee herd owners. These developments represent significant changes with implications for pastoral institution building. The Malian scenario is similar to the situations in the other countries.

The Niger delta plays a vital role in sustaining pastoralism in Mali, in the project area in particular, by providing dry season grazing for several months of the year. The inner delta covers 18,000 sq. km. and has a population of about 220,000 consisting of several ethnic groups.

Peuls, the traditional livestock raisers, are dominant. Their Jooros, the traditional Peul chiefs, control the most important bourgou grasslands. Peul and Tuareg herders move into the delta with their herds in October/November and move out in May/June as the rainy season begins. The grazing area in the delta continues to shrink because of agricultural expansion while the livestock population has been steadily regenerating after the drought and under the impact of the animal health services on the project. Partly with the assistance of donor grants, the project has developed valuable technical knowledge on the regeneration of bourgou grassland, and has achieved a regeneration of 10,000 square kilometers with active local participation. The carrying capacity of the delta has been dramatically exceeded leading to overgrazing of the shrinking grasslands. The delta's importance to the sustainability of pastoralism, its high potential for agriculture and fishing, and the resultant conflicts of interest are all reminders of the need for a more rational and integrated approach to the management of delta resources.

PO formation and mobilization

The PO formation process in Mali started in 1985 with the second phase of the livestock project. One major aim of the project was to rationalize resource use by establishing POs and granting them the necessary rights and assistance to manage their land and water resources.

There are two types of pastoral organizations within the overall project; pastoral cooperatives (PCs) and pastoral associations (PAs). The former, set up under the Cooperative Law, have a longer history. Exclusively established for activities like animal fattening and marketing, they are not defined with reference to range and water resources. The pastoral associations are sponsored by the project and are defined with reference to water points and space. They can also undertake the same activities as PCs. This paper discusses the PAs. There are no project-sponsored POs in the Niger delta.

When ODEM was set up in 1975 to implement the livestock development project, it was expected to be given sufficient authority by the government to adjudicate conflicts of tenure and resource use. Activating pastoralists and forming them into POs was one of its tasks. According to ODEM's sociologist, the original concept was a three-tier PO beginning at the local level with voluntary groups of ten families each, several of which would unite to form a pastoral cell. Several such cells would combine to form a PA or unité pastorale (UP). The philosophy was that the pastoralists should take the initiative to form the voluntary groups, while ODEM would promote the process by increasing awareness of the need, and later play a more active role in formalizing the PAs and granting them water and land rights. The mobilization of pastoralists did not take place according to this vision. Not a single PO was formalized before 1980.

A main reason for the slow progress is that ODEM justified changing the original idea of PO formation preceding construction of water points, on the ground that some quick benefits would help motivate the pastoralists to join POs. This disregarded the idea of mobilizing the pastoralists first and making them active partners of ODEM in selecting the locations for permanent water points. The well and borehole construction exercise then ran into serious technical and logistical problems because of inadequate hydrological data, mis-identification of locations in farming areas, cost escalation, and administrative bottle-necks.

ODEM's field staff lacked professional competence in assisting pastoralists to organize themselves, their competence being almost entirely in animal health. There are two sociologists with a staff of thirteen at the headquarters in Mopti. No competent field staff have been permanently stationed in the field to organize and train pastoralists. ODEM also lacked personnel who spoke the languages of the pastoralists.

The government failed to delegate authority to ODEM to deal with land rights and administrative matters. Nor did the government provide adequate amounts of counterpart funds in time, or vehicles for the field operations.

By the end of 1990, 35 PAs had been formally established. The total membership, entirely male, is less than 3,000, or 3 percent of the targeted beneficiaries of 100,000 pastoral families. In fact, the vast majority of the target population is still outside the formal structure of PAs.

The spatial delineation of PAs has not been completed. Many PAs do not know their spatial limits. Of the five PAs visited only two knew their boundaries. The other three had a vague idea of their territory. The record of PO development looks unimpressive given the period of existence of the project, in contrast to ODEM's achievements in animal health and herd regeneration.

Herd regeneration. Success in herd regeneration was accompanied by dramatic changes in ownership because of dispossession of pastoralists by richer pastoralists and non-pastoralists such as traders, farmers and civil servants. The levels of dispossession and absentee herd ownership are high enough to create serious obstacles to pastoral institution building and NRM.

Food security

The majority of the herders are now partly or fully dependent on a wage relationship. In theory, there are three possibilities to enhance their entitlements. One is by reconstituting their own herds to levels that ensure at least their subsistence. For this they need credit support which is not available at present. Another is by getting their employers to pay them better wages in cash or in kind. This would require the PO to play a trade union role which it cannot. The third way is to strengthen their own food production. This risks the uncertainties of both weather and pests. Any viable approach to improve food security has to operate on all three fronts.

The food security situation seems more precarious in the Mema region where many families do not own cattle. One traditional arrangement that seems to be working is exchanging water for milk with transhuming herders. The transhuming herders leave a few cows with the PAs which distribute the milk among their members.

Cereal banks. Pastoralists believe that livestock prices are low, leading to low food purchasing power in the dry season. The problem is also related to the dynamic nature of the terms of trade. The concept of cereal banks gained currency in the project area as a means to acquire food and enhance food security, although functioning cereal banks have yet to become a reality in many PAs. The main problem is the lack of a revolving fund which reflects the difficulties of the PAs in getting institutional loans, as well as their own organizational deficiencies. Cereal banks are operational in a few PAs with support from NGOs and the World Food Program. Two PAs (Kita and Karawassa) received loans from the National Agricultural Development Bank (BNDA) to establish cereal banks and for animal fattening. Kita and some other PAs in the Mema area attempted to establish their cereal banks by each collectively cultivating five square kilometers of grains. In the past two years, however, there were total crop failures due to insect damage, a major permanent threat to crop production. They are now hoping to get food aid from relief agencies. The pest problem has added another formidable risk factor to grain production which already suffers from the low and unreliable rainfall in the highlands.

ODEM does not encourage food production in the highlands. One official stated that the Tuaregs should practice only pure pastoralism. But the Tuaregs say they do not have enough animals to do this. One of their leaders said: "Our settling down in a fixed place was like a forced landing. The droughts forced us to settle and we felt that agro-pastoralism was less risky than pure pastoralism." But in the present context, with the major pest problem, agriculture in the highlands has become doubly risky.

An NGO has mobilized agro-pastoralists in Duenza to establish and successfully run cereal banks. This scheme covers 70 villages with a staff of twelve. It lends capital to village-level associations to buy grains for their cereal banks soon after harvests when prices are low. The food is sold in the dry season at a small profit but still below the market price. The expatriate anthropologist heading the project said: "Now, they are making substantial profits. Their overhead is low, so they can sell at a reasonable price and still make a profit. Cereal banks can work with a modest initial subsidy and may be a way to build POs." This is an experience worth studying. It is also worth looking at the experiences of PCs that have been successful in setting-up their own revolving funds.

Resource security

Regarding the major tenurial issues of water availability, a recent study (Cissé 1991) has concluded that the existing waterpoints in the highlands can meet pastoralists' needs. Only 15 percent of the project area is outside the reach of a permanent waterpoint, and this can be grazed in the wet season. Even this positive situation has not, however, been achieved with equanimity. ODEM constructed about 65 boreholes and 11 wells, with PAs sharing the costs of many with ODEM. PAs also supplied labor. Other waterpoints were constructed by PAs with 100 percent financial assistance from independently operating foreign donors such as the European Development Fund. Because these donors did not insist on cost-sharing, PAs were attracted by this option, although not all of them succeeded in getting such grants. The foreign donor intervention raised the hopes of many PAs but failed to fulfil them. It also fuelled resentment against ODEM's scheme of cost-sharing. The two schemes should have been coordinated and should have adopted, a common format of cost-sharing.

A continuing problem is waterpoint management by the PAs. Although PAs have well and borehole management committees that levy water charges, none of the five PAs visited had a surplus to meet the cost of major repairs or pump replacement, although running costs were covered. Some boreholes do not have pumps, causing water scarcity and overgrazing around the functioning waterpoints. Well and borehole management is seriously hampered by the unresolved problem of land rights. In Boni, the President complained of outside herders moving into their dry season grazing area in the rainy season, against the rules set by the PA.

PAs do not have any management plans or grazing schemes: although the pastoralists recognize the need to stabilize sand dunes, and protect and plant trees, practical action is limited. Firebreaks are conspicuous by their absence. In Boni, the sole firebreak has not been cleared for some time, and extensive damage has been caused by a recent bushfire. Some PAs have formed range brigades for patrolling but are hindered by lack of camel transport. While the lack of secure land rights and the incomplete spatial delineation of PAs are major disincentives to sustainable NRM, of no less importance is the lack of management skills at the PA level.

Importance of the delta

The special importance of the Niger delta to the sustainability of livestock production must be fully recognized. The second phase of the project was expected to address integration of crop-livestock production in the delta. However, it appears that the ORM-ODEM relationship was not based on any jointly and systematically evolved principles of cooperation. With the ORM intervention, intersectoral conflicts increased because of land conversion to rice production and blocking of transhumant cattle paths by rice fields. ORM's activities are confined only to a part of the rice areas and its performance in terms of rice yields and costs of production leaves much to be desired. In 1990, of the 28,000 ha planted, only 4,700 ha were harvested.

At present there are no formal institutional links between the POs in the highlands and possible counterpart or cooperating institutions in the delta. In fact, the issue has not been addressed either by the Malian Government or the project. Many a pastoralist spends more than 10,000 CFA per head of cattle to gain entry into the delta and access to the privately owned bourgou grass, often paying to several Jooros. The Jooros have lost considerable traditional credibility by selling land-use rights to local farmers and city dwellers, often with the support of the local government. Some mechanism is needed to regulate access and land-use in ways that can help accumulate funds for the sustainable management of the delta as a whole.

The significance of herd ownership

Neither ODEM nor the Malian Government has recognized the predominance of absentee herd ownership as a major issue affecting pastoral institution building for sustainable NRM. Absentee herd owners are not pastoralists and therefore are not involved in the affairs of PAs. Their main occupations are trade, the civil service, and farming. They are not likely to be seriously concerned with problems like range and water management. Even if they see the importance of NRM, they are not likely to become involved in it. Absentee herd owners favor open access rangelands so that their herds can graze anywhere. They may even use their political influence to prevent PAs receiving legally defensible land rights. Their herders, on the other hand, working for a wage, are fully engaged in herding. The pressure of work, their low social status, and the fact that the animals they are herding are not their own demotivate them from becoming involved in NRM.

PA leaders were very reluctant to discuss ownership patterns in detail, although all admitted that there was a high degree of absentee ownership. In the absence of institutional support, there are hardly any viable means of herd reconstitution for the individual pastoralist. Many went to the delta and towns and even abroad (some to Burkina in search of gold) with the will to earn money, come back with it, buy animals and become herd owners again. But of those who went with these hopes, said a pastoralist in Boni, "not even one in a hundred came back with money enough to buy a minimum number of animals". Cattle theft by dispossessed herders is reportedly on the increase, though this is not an entirely new practice among Peul and other pastoral societies. An official in the delta said "nowadays cattle theft is a more serious problem than animal disease." While he may have exaggerated, pauperization has driven many a herder to stealing cattle for survival.

Services

Animal health. This has been the most important service provided by the project and the people's awareness of animal health problems and solutions is remarkable. The veterinary services have played an important role in herd regeneration; the major animal diseases are under control. There are 35 veterinary posts, 145 vaccination parks, and 212 field workers trained in animal health in the whole project area including the delta. However, there are logistical problems due to lack of transport for the field staff and the long distances pastoralists have to take their animals to a veterinary post. Evidently, ODEM has not utilized animal health as a rallying point for PO development. Drug distribution is in the hands of private pharmacies and the veterinarians in the field. The PAs participation in managing animal health services is marginal. There are no plans to set up revolving funds at the PA level to supply animal drugs and generate net revenue for the PA.

Literacy. All five PAs visited are operating literacy programs started in 1988-89. Participation is generally low and irregular; though fewer than men, some women are attending. Literacy among PA leaders is low; on the average about 25 percent of PA members are literate. The literacy program is an essential service which needs to be sustained and expanded.

Marketing. At present pastoralists are entirely dependent on private intermediaries for marketing-buyers. There are seasonal fluctuations in livestock prices. The main sources of demand are local farmers, farmer-traders, civil servants and national and regional cattle traders. Most cattle are sold in the hot season in spite of the low prices because of the pastoralists' need for grains at that time (Swift 1985). Although livestock prices are higher in the rainy season, livestock sales are relatively low, because of the reduced cash needs of pastoralists when they can supplement their cereal diet with fresh milk. During the rainy reason, many herders are also busy cultivating small plots of grains and vegetables, and potential buyers, like the farmer-traders, are also occupied in their fields. There are no active institutional arrangements to promote export of livestock. PAs might be able to protect pastoralists' interests if they had a regional or project-level body to promote domestic and export livestock marketing. However, organizations to promote export cannot play any effective role to counter the lowering of export prices caused by the dumping of cheap meat in the region by the European Community.

Leadership and management

All the PAs are dominated by traditional chiefs and their close relatives. This may be inevitable in the early phases, and not necessarily undesirable if the leaders have the imagination, competence, and will to see the new organizational challenges and the needs of the pastoralists. In the absence of any systematic program by ODEM to develop the new leadership and technical skills, leadership capacities depend on the existing competence and commitment of the traditional leaders. Only a few traditional leaders are, however, already equipped with adequate knowledge and confidence. Of the five PAs studied, the Presidents of only two had sufficient education, self-confidence, and motivation to play their roles effectively. Even these two lacked a coterie with the basic technical awareness of aspects of NRM such as construction of firebreaks or tree conservation, or in law, and governmental and ODEM affairs, and financial management. The lack of a core of members with these skills may lead to a lack of confidence to undertake NRM and new revenue-generating activities. The need for management training is clear; the main barrier is the low level of literacy. Thus the traditional leaders continue in power irrespective of their competence and their contribution to the progress of the PAs. ODEM should promote the development of alternate leadership through a more intensive literacy and management training program.

Economic viability

At present the only revenue-generating activity common to all PAs is collection of water charges. None of the five PAs reported any accumulation of surplus. Not all the PAs collect membership fees. There is no standard procedure for membership. Some PAs have introduced a membership fee, but animal taxes collected by traditional chiefs (who are also leaders of PAs) go to the national coffers. PAs are not authorized to collect taxes. Nor are they entitled to receive any part of the taxes collected from their members by the chiefs. In general, the lack of revenue makes the PA's economic viability very low. Lack of revenue-generating activities leads to lack of economic viability which in turn makes it impossible to start new activities. Ways have to be found to break out of this vicious circle. More efficient management of water points to raise revenue, more regular membership fees, a more active mobilization of members and credit schemes for revolving funds for new profitable activities are among the means.

Reasons for lack of progress

Reasons for the project's failure to show satisfactory progress in PO-building seem to be: (a) lack of an adequate number of competent and committed field personnel to animate and organize the intended beneficiaries; (b) failure to monitor and review the PO-formation process at early stages and take appropriate steps to solve problems with due consideration to issues like herders' entitlements and food security (this may be a reflection of a lack of innovative minds at the higher levels of the project); (c) failure to develop institutional linkages between PAs in the highlands and their possible counterparts in the Niger delta; (d) failure of the government to delegate authority to ODEM to grant land rights and to adjudicate resource-use conflicts (the ministry concerned was not in favor of ODEM undertaking any tasks other than veterinary activities); and (e) failure of the government to fulfil its other commitments to the projects (timely release of counterpart funds and purchase of vehicles for the field services); and (f) lack of adequate supervision of PO formation and NRM activities at field level by experts.

The situation calls for a thorough review of ODEM's competence to deal with the challenge of pastoral institution building for NRM and of the role of the government in providing the legal framework for communal land and water rights, and the resources to support PO development in the long term. The government should be willing to strengthen the adult education and human health facilities in the pastoral areas. The issue of absentee herd ownership should be addressed for reasons of social justice as well as sustainable NRM.

Mauritania

Under review is the Second Livestock Project (1987-92) successor to the First Livestock Development Project (1971-79). The objectives of the project are to slow the deterioration of the grazing area and to boost productivity by making groups of pastoralists (pastoral associations or PAs) responsible for allocated grazing areas, and to provide better services and production inputs. Institutional and structural reforms are additional aims of the project, which was to establish fifteen PAs on a pilot basis.

The main project beneficiaries are the approximately 180,000 Moors and some Peul who are pastoral and agro-pastoral people in an area of 130,000 square kilometers in the Trarza, Brakna, and Gorgol Provinces in the southern parts of Mauritania.

The traditional territorial organizations of the Moors are based on lineage or class. Membership of a specified group confers rights to pasture in the territory of that group. Traditionally dominant groups excluded other groups or made them pay tribute for access to pasture (Swift 1988). There are distinct caste structures within Moor societies, which traditionally held "domestic servants". The Peul are late arrivals in the area and had no traditional rights to land.

Peul societies are much less hierarchical than those of the Moors. Although weakened over the last decades, the traditional systems still determine the broad pattern of spatial distribution of pastoral and agro-pastoral groups in the project area.

During the drought years of the 1970s and 1980s several hundred thousand pastoralists migrated to the main cities and to Senegal—or settled around permanent water points or oases, leading a trend towards agro-pastoralism in the rural and peri-urban areas. While about 60 percent of the total population were nomadic pastoralists in the 1960s, today less than 10 percent would fall into that category (Bonte personal communication).

Around the new pastoral settlements, problems of overgrazing, loss of trees, and land degradation are becoming increasingly serious. Such resource degradation is significant in the project area, and is most pronounced in the more densely populated south-western parts and in the interior to Nouakchott. Around Mederdra and Rosso and along the coastal road to Nouakchott are large areas with moving sand dunes, many of them rolling over settlements and agricultural fields.

Faced with a serious economic crisis, the government has adopted a policy of privatization of the livestock sector, encouraging private individuals and institutions (POs) to assume greater responsibilities for livestock development activities. Policy levels have thus been compelled to address pastoral institution building as a serious issue. This provides an opportunity for POs to take greater responsibility for NRM and thereby strengthen their legitimacy with respect to land and water rights, and participate in the privatization of animal health services by setting-up their own pharmacies and other services.

PO formation and mobilization

The project started in 1987 and by January 1988 the first PAs were identified by using socio-economic and environmental data. The PAs were based partly on the traditional organizations, and partly on new organizations. About 20 days were spent over a period of one year on visiting all villages and camps, electing village delegates, calling a general assembly with all the delegates and electing the board of each new PA. A two-tier model of POs was chosen, the lower level being the village or camp PO consisting of groups of 10 to 20 families. A management committee was elected for each village PO. The average PA covers 50 villages, 2,500 sq. km and a population of about 14,000 people. The average number of livestock per PA is 12,500 cattle, 36,000 sheep and goats, 5,000 camels, and 4,000 horses and donkeys.

Implementation of the PA component progressed faster than envisaged. In two years 14 of the 15 target PAs had been established. Reasons for the successful implementation were a well-designed approach, prompt recruitment of competent project staff, appropriate technical assistance, a hard-working project team with good backing from the project management, and good timing of the intervention. The hardships suffered during the droughts had made the pastoralists increasingly aware of the fragile nature of their environment and production systems, and of the need for better access to government services. A competent and relatively well-educated leadership of the existing pastoral institutions see the PAs as potential tools for strengthening their own positions and the positions of the pastoralists in general in relation to the government. There is a mutual understanding between the government and the pastoralists and their leaders about what services the government is realistically able to provide.

Some problems became evident in forming the PAs. The 20 days for establishing one PA left only a few hours for meetings and discussions in each village—too short a time for any real participation of the pastoralists to take place. The territory under each PA is very large (2,500 sq. km) and may seriously hinder communication between the villages. The population under each PA is also too high - averaging

13,700—ranging from 3,000 to 25,000 people—to ensure satisfactory membership participation in decisionmaking.

Despite the commitment of the project team, the approach had a strong top-down character and the first people to be mobilized were the traditional leaders and in some cases a few of the more literate younger men around them. The village or the settlement level should have been more consciously addressed as the basic building block of the PA at the initial stage. The project team has become aware of this need and the village now receives greater emphasis at the conceptual level.

Some of the PAs found to be too large were divided into two. PA boundaries were also adjusted to match administrative boundaries, although according to Bonte, who was actively involved as a consultant in the project's PO activities, it was difficult to limit the territories because of close kinship ties (personal communication). The issue of optimum size of PAs remains unresolved. While a PA large in area and population may be necessary for range management, it may be less efficient in management of water points, credit schemes, economic affairs, literacy, and training programs, for which the village level is a more effective basic unit.

Other implementation problems which affect or are likely to affect progress are:

- The inefficient financial and daily management of BIE, the agency responsible for credit, distribution, and sales of veterinary drugs to the PAs.
- Delays in tendering and procurement of vehicles and components for water development.
- Delays of government funding to the livestock services causing severe liquidity problems for the project and strain on day-to-day operations.
- Delays in posting of new field extension officers.

Food security

The food security of the pastoralists in the project area fell considerably during the drought years because of loss and dispossession of animals. Although aimed at improving herd management and marketing, the project could also support reconstitution of herds through credit, but so far has not done so. The establishment of the PAs has to some extent improved food security through provision of revolving fund credit for milk and meat-producing units, vegetable gardens, and basic supplies such as sugar. These activities are not widespread, however, and have a very modest impact. On the other hand, the agricultural activities around the ponds, oases and new settlements are of growing importance in the local economies, but suffer from the low and unreliable rainfall. A major challenge for the project will be to promote functional integration of the crop cultivation with livestock and tree production and management, combined with water harvesting and conservation measures. The PAs and village POs could become local centers for training, extension and exchange of local skills in agro-sylvo-pastoral production.

Resource security and management

A condition of the project loan was that the government would grant the PAs usufruct rights to rangeland. The relevant government department (Ministre de l'Intérieur) delayed until 14 August 1990 the issue of a circular recognizing the PAs' right to manage the rangeland and providing the PAs with priority rights to water and grazing resources within the PA boundaries. The presidents of PAs reviewed expressed discontent about this delay. Although they acknowledged that the circular was an important first step, they insisted that supplementary regulatory texts for each PA would be needed if they were to exercise adequate authority on land-use matters.

The lack of water is a major constraint to human and livestock development in the project area. Large rangeland areas around Bassikounou, for example, are without water points and remain underutilized. Water availability varies within the project area. In Monguel PA, there are 560 wells and 830 registered ponds, while in Mederdra there are only 36 and 6 respectively. The average number of wells per PA is 250 to 300. The project policy is to provide each PA with one new well and to rehabilitate four wells. The wells are private, public, and communal. During the First Livestock Development Project (1971-79), water development was a major component and many public wells were rehabilitated and constructed. As in the other projects, the public wells, by their open access nature, made the rangeland around them an open access resource too. Hence, this form of expansion of water points had severe negative effects on range management.

As a result of these negative experiences, the new project took a different approach. Only legally-recognized PAs would have rights to wells, and the PAs and village POs would establish management committees with responsibility for well management. A formally organized, functioning well management system is crucial for the management of the rangeland. The PAs are expected to contribute 10 percent of the financial cost in cash or kind for water development. The government is also permitting local POs to take over the management of public wells and boreholes. Since the water development component of the project is far behind schedule, there is little experience with these new management committees.

Environmental degradation and land-use conflicts are increasing in the project area and its vicinity. Conflicts between pastoralists and cultivators over land-use, and the introduction of new land tenure laws caused the recent conflicts in the Senegal River Valley leading to the closing of the border between Senegal and Mauritania. No clear delineations between agricultural areas and grazing land exist within the PAs. A national law requires that agriculturalists guard their fields during the day and herders watch over their animals at night. But conflicts are still frequent during periods of pasture scarcity. Conflicts that cannot be resolved at PA levels are referred to the Department of Livestock and the local government administration.

Some improvement in rainfall in the last few years may explain the vegetation regeneration in certain areas, but environmental degradation is a problem with serious local and regional implications. A major initial achievement of PO formation is its contribution to increased environmental awareness by pastoralists and PA leaders. However, this impressive consciousness has yet to be translated into action in the form of range management plans or grazing schemes. Prevention of tree-cutting and effective control of bushfires have taken place in some PAs around village centers, but not on a complete PA-wide scale. The many firebreaks constructed in the 1970s have not been maintained.

There is apparent contradiction between the 14 August circular and the dominant interpretation of Islamic law (shari'a). The circular gives the PAs the right to deny outsiders access to PA rangeland when pasture is scarce and overgrazed. But Islamic law as well as local custom will make it difficult for PAs to deny others such access. Only local regulations can provide local PO leaders with sufficient authority to impose some control on grazing, for example by the stock of absentee herd owners.

Several unsuccessful tree-planting projects and attempts to stabilize sand dunes were seen. The restoration of the old firebreaks and the creation of new would require planning, labor, and materials. At present the PAs are not adequately equipped financially for such tasks. The introduction of new NRM activities must be based on careful cost-benefit assessments and introduced through participatory approaches.

Herd ownership

Both Moor and Peul pastoralists have lost large shares of their livestock through sale to absentee herd owners. As much as 40 percent of the livestock in the project is said to belong to absentee owners. It seems that neither the project management nor the Mauritanian government recognizes that dispossession of animals has severe consequences the for the socio-economic security of pastoral households, and that the increase in absentee ownership has major implications for NRM and pastoral institution building. Many of the same problems outlined in the review of Mali are also present in Mauritania.

The abolition of animal taxes since the droughts of 1984-85 and the introduction of property taxes have given further impetus to absentee ownership. Many richer people in the towns prefer to invest in cattle instead of in real estate. Absentee herd owners in Mauritania are mainly concentrated in Nouakchott and a few other towns. They prefer to keep their herds as close as possible to their towns; for instance, the bulk of the herds belonging to owners living in Nouakchott are found within a radius of 100 kilometers around the city. Such concentration of herds in limited areas contributes to overgrazing and exacerbates land-use conflicts around the towns.

Services

Animal health. This is the main component of the project which has built an efficient service building on achievements during the First Livestock Development Project 1971-79. Most of the livestock is vaccinated through the annual campaign, which is the main operation of the Livestock Department. The major animal diseases are under control. The service is well appreciated and used by the pastoralists. Veterinary drugs are sold at the field posts, but pastoralists complain that the supplies are often inadequate and the posts too far apart. Following the new policy of privatization, several private drug stores have been opened in most towns, but they are still too few in the rural areas. A main benefit of membership in joining the PAs is access to veterinary drugs from PA stores.

Veterinary drug stores have been established by PAs with revolving funds in nine of the fourteen PAs. The PA board members and the village delegates collect a minimum of 100 Ugyia per person as a membership fee and contribution to the revolving fund. None of the PA presidents reported particular problems in raising these funds. Some people paid considerably higher amounts to the fund. The project adds 100 percent to the funds collected by the PA for the first stock of veterinary drugs. The PAs appoint a shopkeeper, who is paid a small amount from the profit of the sales. So far profits have been low because of high transportation costs, and the government policy of keeping veterinary drug prices uniform throughout the country. The presidents have, however, been able to negotiate a change in this policy, and profits from the drug stores may improve. Since the veterinary drug stores have been opened recently, it is too early to assess how efficiently they are being operated.

Extension has in the past been an integral part of the animal health service with a narrow focus on animal health and husbandry. The project has financed a broadening of the training program for extension staff at the Kaedi School of Agriculture, where the students are now trained for three years in all aspects of agro-sylvo-pastoral production and resource management. The first young officers took up their posts this year. They appear to be theoretically well prepared for their tasks, although, of course, lacking practical experience. There will only be one or two extension staff posted to each PA. Since they will compete with the general animal service and the vaccination campaign for transport and petrol, there is a risk that they will not be able to operate efficiently. Only one female extension officer is with the project.

The project also trains pastoral agents through a mobile unit and at the field posts. Some fifteen pastoral agents, chosen from village delegates, have been trained. The main focus of training has been on animal health. Pastoral agents will work with the PAs and are expected to be remunerated by them. They receive no fixed government salaries.

Marketing. Credit has been provided for animal fattening and milk producing units. The main domestic market for surplus production has been the urban areas, in particular Nouakchott. The main export market has been through transhumance to Senegal and coastal West African countries through Mali. The pastoralists are dependant on private traders and individual sales, and to a lesser extent on SOMECOB for marketing. SOMECOB is an inefficient state body with a monopoly on livestock exports which in practice is able to market only a minor share of total exports. There are no other institutional arrangements to promote marketing in the project area. Marketing is further constrained by long distances and bad road systems, a fall in domestic demand and low meat prices, and lately by the closing of the Senegalese border. A livestock marketing study is being prepared and should be able to identify what role the PAs, the project and the government could play in protecting the interests of the pastoralists in marketing.

Literacy. Although many Koranic schools exist locally, the general literacy in Arabic is probably less than 10 percent. The literacy level among women is even lower. Since the project does not envisage operating any literacy program, it should encourage links between the PA component and on-going national literacy programs.

Human health. Human health is not part of the project or PA activities, although it is a high priority of the pastoralists.

Leadership and management

The PO boards are all dominated by traditional Moor leaders, often elders from the nobility. This is not necessarily undesirable if they have appropriate skills and leadership competence. A few younger and better-educated men have replaced less dynamic board members in some PAs. There are no women among the PA board members. Most of the leaders are fully literate in Arabic and several are also literate in French. A few of the presidents were former teachers, traders, or entrepreneurs with skills in economic planning and management. The competence and commitment of the six presidents met was impressive, indicating high potential to play their roles as PA leaders. But the leadership competence varies from one PA to another and there is clearly a need for a management training program. Training is needed in all aspects of natural resources management including sand dune stabilization, tree protection, and management of firebreaks. Training is also needed for the board members of women's groups.

Achievements. Although PO formation process in Mauritania has been going on for less than two years, it has already contributed to an increased awareness of environmental degradation. The PAs are involved in a variety of economic activities such as veterinary drug sales and milk and meat production schemes. The PAs have partly strengthened the traditional pastoral institutions and partly formed a new institutional basis for resource management and development. The PAs are open to everyone, and provide credit and training opportunities to all members. The lower castes and the "domestic servants" have, however, very little influence in PA decisionmaking and benefit less from PA activities. This is also their position within the traditional institutions. The main benefit of the PO formation may lie in its mobilization of pastoralists into a growing political movement. This is an unintended outcome of the PO formation, although it seems to receive government attention and even some degree of support. Competent PA leaders have started to articulate the pastoralists common interests at regional and national levels.

Some of the more dynamic PA leaders have been campaigning for a National Herders Association. Five of the presidents have drafted a preliminary constitution for such an organization. A first general assembly is soon to be held. This is a clear indication of a political process from below and the project's institution building initiative, though originated from above, has been the main stimulus.

Economic viability

The main revenue-generating activities of the PAs are the collection of membership charges and the accumulation of surplus from the sale of drugs, (until now small or non-existent). Some PAs collect water charges, others pool camels or livestock for milk sales or fattening. The PAs are not involved in collecting taxes or fines for such activities as illegal tree-cutting.

Economic performance varies from one PA to another and economic viability is still low. But they have been in existence for only a couple of years. Potentials for more profitable economic activities lie in more regular collection of membership fees, expanded credit schemes, sale of veterinary drugs, and improved livestock production and marketing.

Problems. Project implementation problems are severely limiting progress in formation and development. Issues to be addressed include:

- Formulation of local regulations on land and water rights.
- Delays in provision of transport and support for extension and training.
- Inadequate attention accorded to competence-building in integrated resource management and pastoral institution building in the Livestock Department and other implementing agencies.
- Lack of female extension officers to train women's group leaders and encourage the participation of women in the mainstream activities of the project.
- Evaluation of the pilot phase of PO formation.
- Adequate planning of the new NRM activities to be initiated in the extension phase.
- Strengthening of the coordination at policy and field level between various sectors involved in the project areas.
- Reinforcement of the Livestock Department and the team responsible for PO formation before embarking upon the goal of establishing 101 more POs across the country. The sociologist who until recently headed the section responsible for the PO formation was replaced by a veterinarian.

Niger

The project under review, PENCE (Project de Développement de l'Elevage au Niger Centre-Est), was a response to the disastrous consequences of the 1969 and 1972-73 droughts on pastoral production and communities. The project was aimed at herd regeneration, redevelopment of the livestock sector, and better management of range and water resources. Demarcation of pastoral units, formation and recognition of POs, and operation of pastoral centers (CPs) to provide services such as human and animal health, grain supplies, and literacy programs were identified as important steps.

The intended beneficiaries included pastoral groups of Tamachek (Tuareg and Bouzou), Toubou (Toubou, Touboshi and Assa), Arab and Peul (Wodaabe and Farfarou). The Tamachek and the Toubou practice transhumance. During the rainy season they leave their pastures and traditional wells in the south and migrate with the livestock to fertile pastures in the north. They have traditional usufruct rights to certain territory based on criteria such as investment in wells and the period of habitation. The Fulani Wodaabe are the most mobile. Often, they are not attached to any particular territory but move in search of water and pasture.

Traditionally, all these pastoral groups practiced very little agriculture. However, as in the other Sahelian countries, a variety of factors including the effects of recurrent droughts have compelled a growing number to opt for a more sedentary way of life with transhumance as the main way to sustain herds. Changes have taken place in herd size, composition and ownership patterns, and an increasing number of households must rely on activities other than livestock-raising for their subsistence.

PENCE was originally intended to cover a total of 324,000 square kilometers or 25 percent of the country in the east-central regions covering Maradi, Zinder and Diffa. Later the activities were concentrated in the pastoral areas of Zinder covering an area of 75,000 square kilometers with a population of 70,000 to 80,000.

PO formation and mobilization

The project was originally planned for the period 1979-84 but had to be extended until 1989 because of disruptions caused by the drought of 1983-84. Three phases in the ten-year history of the project are start-up, 1979-83; retraction, 1983-85; and recovery and full operation, 1985-89. The project is currently receiving temporary financial support from the French CCCE to continue some of its activities including PO development.

The Nigerien project addressed pastoral institution building in a systematic and sustained way, although its progress has been slow and the future is uncertain. Before project establishment, there was considerable discussion within the livestock ministry and between the ministry and the donors including the World Bank on the approach to PO formation and land and water rights. A detailed study provided valuable information on some of the lesser known socio-economic aspects of pastoralism in the project area including mobility patterns, and provided insights into pastoralists' perceptions of their organizational needs. After the 1983-84 drought, the project leadership became more conscious of the high priority pastoralists gave to food security, animal and human health and resource security and their awareness of the importance of literacy in a modern context. The project specialists competent in community development were stationed in the field, and the veterinary personnel were interested and involved in pastoral institution building.

The pastoral organization consists of three levels, with the GMPs (Groupement Mutualiste Pastoraux) as the basic units, the GVC (Groupement a Vocation Cooperative) as the intermediate level composed of seven or eight GMPs, and the CP (Centre Pastoraux) as the apex body made up of a number of GVCs. The GMP is the unit for water management and collective water rights to GMP wells formerly public. The GVC deals with rangeland management, communal land rights, and cooperative shops, and the CP with overall administration and provision of services like animal and human health, literacy, and management training. Each CP is headed by a center manager who is a junior livestock specialist, with a staff consisting of a community development worker with competence in cooperation (*animateur*), a nurse, a veterinary technician, and auxiliary workers such as drivers, laborers, and guards. Of the six CPs planned under the project, five have been established.

So far, 147 GMPs and nine GVCs have been established. About 60 percent of the GMPs have been incorporated into GVCs. About 19 more GVCs are scheduled to be established under the CPs. The first GMPs were created in 1982, but the drought of 1983-84 disrupted the GMP formation process until 1985. The GMPs were formed mainly on the basis of tribes and around common water points or with the understanding that common waterpoints will be acquired. Present average membership per GMP is about 40. In membership campaigns conducted by the *animateurs*, the conversion of public water points into collective possessions of GMPs and the promise of cooperative shops to supply provisions, of human and animal health services, and of literacy programs were major inducements for the pastoralists to accept the GMPs and the structure built on them.

Membership dilemma

In spite of the campaigns at the local level by the *animateurs* with active support from the other field staff at the CP, the project has not been able to mobilize more than 30 percent of the potential GMP members. This may not be a poor record in view of tensions between the project and the Nigerien government. There were changes in project leadership. The government delayed legislation to formalize water and land rights. There are special problems in organizing GMPs for the nomadic Wodaabe who are always on the move. However, the basic problem is the lack of a clear concept of membership by which to distinguish a member from a non-member within a local group, or to identify advantages exclusive to a member. This problem is not unique to the Nigerien project. In a typical case, a GMP is formed on the basis of a tribal sub-group, but not all the members of the sub-group need to become members of the GMP for it to be assigned collective water rights. Nevertheless, all of them, members and non-members alike, enjoy the collective right to the well. A GMP member is said to be entitled to a card. However, there is no prescribed membership fee although a few GMPs have collected a contribution of 500 CFA each from some of their members.

A significant omission in both the original project design and the revised approach is the role of women in pastoral production and resource management. As in the other countries, women have been totally excluded.

Food security

During the 1983-84 drought, many groups in the project area migrated to distant places in search of food, water, and pasture. Along the way, they lost animals to death and distress sale. Several groups ended up in Nigeria and have not yet returned. Since the drought, only a minority of pastoralists have been able to regenerate their own herds to viable pre-drought levels. The forms of gift and credit systems traditional in the pastoral societies—such as the Peuls' Habani system—have either fallen into disuse or proved inadequate against the magnitude of livestock loss and destitution, although the traditional survival strategies can be efficient tools during minor droughts when the number of families in need of help is limited. After the drought, a herd reconstitution credit scheme was introduced, but did not make a significant impact.

Today only a few pastoralists in the project area are able to meet their subsistence needs solely from traditional livestock keeping. In the region, there are very few other income-making opportunities such as seasonal labor migration, herd tenancy for non-traditional livestock owners (farmers, officials and urban dwellers) and crop production on marginal soils. Even these alternative activities are often insufficient to ensure a household's needs. The net result is frequently that an already small family herd is continuously diminishing as the family must barter or sell their livestock for cereals, until the family becomes impoverished.

Cooperative shops. After the drought, the project took a significant step to increase food availability below market prices by setting up cooperative shops at the GVC level. This was a move on the part of the project to use food availability as a tool to mobilize pastoralists. By the end of 1989, ten cooperative shops had been opened with revolving funds provided by external donors, the ILO and the WFP being the major sources of finance and initial food stocks respectively. The latter contributed nine tons of cereals to each shop. Some of the cooperatives have since been closed because of mismanagement, but others are functioning satisfactorily.

The shop at Tejira was established in 1986 with a revolving fund of about 900,000 CFA from ILO. The cooperative buys food and other essentials in bulk, as far as possible when their prices are low, and sells them to pastoralists below market prices but still keeping a margin. Grains are purchased in the agro-pastoral and agricultural zones during harvest seasons. The shop has been well managed and its revolving fund had expanded to 2.25 million CFA by the end of 1990. Many GMP leaders and members in the Tejra area counted the cooperative as an important benefit. The shop is managed by a committee of six members including a representative from the CP staff. A shop assistant is employed for its daily running. The shop has proved its economic viability as it is now self-sustaining. The success of the shop's management owes a lot to the dedication of the CP staff who continue to play an active role in helping and supervising the management committee.

Such intervention from the CP staff may be needed for a long time before the pastoralist members become entirely self-sufficient in the basic skills needed to manage the shop efficiently.

The extension of cooperative shops to the whole project area depends on the availability of external support for the revolving fund, and the managerial skills among members at the GVC level. Another important requirement is the commitment of the CP staff to making the cooperative shop a successful venture by giving the necessary training and supervision to the management committee.

Resource security

There is no legal restriction on herders' access to pastures. However, indirect control is possible by individuals and groups (GMPs) who own or control waterpoints. The 16 GMP wells are a recent creation awaiting full legalization. The public wells made pastures available that were formerly unexploited because of lack of water, but as open access resources they became overgrazed. Pastoralists met during research had definite views on the relationship between the GMP and the traditional wells, and on land rights including tree tenure. They support the conversion of public, open access, water points into GMP possessions. They also support more clearly defined and legally defensible communal usufruct rights to land which accommodates their need for spatial mobility and the traditions of reciprocity between different communities in range and water use. The *Code Rurale* reflects these sentiments of the pastoralists.

Traditional wells in the area are privately owned and managed by pastoral families and clans. These private rights are recognized and respected by the community, and are legally defensible. The ownership of wells gives their owners some degree of indirect control over the surrounding pastures, although custom and the ecology of Sahelian pastoralism preclude monopolistic control. Members of the local community enjoy priority over outsiders in access to private wells. In return, the well owner receives labor from the local community for the upkeep of the well. The traditional well needs frequent de-silting and replacement of the wooden lining. These are labor-intensive operations. Normally an outsider is allowed free access to a traditional well for only about three days and if sufficient grass is available. After this period of free access, some form of payment or gift in kind must be offered to the well-owner. The payment is invariably in labor for the upkeep of the well or for watering the owner's animals. The gift is often in small ruminants. The transaction is actually determined according the interpersonal relationship that develops between the well-owner and the outsider-user. Rigid management of private wells is limited by the tradition of reciprocity among pastoral communities and the ecological determinants of pastoral production in the Sahel. Given the low, erratic and unevenly distributed rainfall and the uncertainties it poses to livestock production, a private well-owner needs to transhume like any other pastoralist to find pasture and water. Most traditional well owners are GMP members.

Initially the project planned to construct 30 concrete wells and water tanks. The project's most important precondition for any well construction was that the Nigerien government assign exclusive rights to each well to one user group—that is, one GMP. The government's reluctance to change its earlier policies concerning water tenure seriously hampered PENCE's water program. In 1983, the target number of water points was reduced to 18 concrete wells to be located mainly in the pastoral areas of Tejira and Yogoum. When the wells were constructed in 1988, the project supplied the materials and technological back-up, while the GMPs contributed the labor. In 1989, 16 wells were operating, all assigned to different GMPs. Each GMP well has a five-member management committee elected by the members. Today the GMPs have had functioning well management committees for one year.

The GMP well management committee is responsible for the regulation of water use and for setting and collecting water charges. In principle, all herders using a GMP well should pay for the water according to the herd size. This principle is, however, not strictly practiced. According to tradition, the animals in a pastoralist's herd should not be counted. Charges are fixed in general terms, people with larger herds paying larger fees, which may vary again according to social considerations. A GMP can restrict outsiders from access to water and to the surrounding pasture. Just like traditional owners, the GMPs allow outsiders free access to GMP wells for only two or three days, after which they have to pay. Many outsiders still do not respect the authority of the GMP and attempt to by-pass it and use the well.

The GMPs with wells have yet to formulate an appropriate system of water charges. At the current level of revenue, a GMP may be able cover immediate costs of materials and minor repairs but will not be able to meet the costs of major repairs and long-term maintenance. Fortunately, the wells are cement-lined and can last longer than the traditional wells before major repairs become necessary, but this is no reason not to tap the revenue-generating potential of GMP wells.

Pastoralists are aware of the consequences of tree-cutting which is a serious problem in many parts of the project area. They attribute range degradation and the loss of trees mainly to past droughts. Some specifically referred to the disappearance of perennial grass species in the past ten to fifteen years. Dead trees are still the major source of firewood but live trees are cut by Tuaregs to obtain live roots for tent construction and by transhuming herders to feed small ruminants. Trees are also cut to construct lining for traditional wells. The wooden lining has to be replaced once every one to three years depending on the soil conditions; each time 300 to 400 trees may be cut for the purpose.

People did not appear to have any confidence in the government's forest conservation department as an agency to protect trees which are legally state property. The project has introduced a technique of lopping branches of trees for fodder without causing permanent damage to the trees. The GMPs are expected to promote this technique through their brigades for environmental protection which have yet to be formed and trained. The brigades are expected to be responsible for tree protection and bushfire control. They are potentially a far more practical and superior alternative to the government's forest guard system because they make the resource users responsible for the policing of the environment.

Herd ownership

As in the other countries, dispossession and herd accumulation by richer pastoralists, and non-pastoralists, and paid herding have increased, although no data are available to ascertain the extent of these changes. The director of the project admitted that herd ownership patterns had changed and there were possibly more absentee herd owners than officially assumed. During the last two decades, Arab, Fulani, Tamachek and Toubou pastoralists have experienced reductions in herd size and important changes in herd composition. There has been a shift from cattle to more drought-resistant species such as camels and small ruminants, especially among the Tobou and Tamachek. Herding for absentee owners is practiced by Wodaabe nomads who are among the most impoverished. Tamachek and Toubou pastoralists seldom herd animals belonging to owners from other ethnic groups.

An experiment in herd reconstitution credit was initiated in 1985-86 with financial assistance from the World Bank and some NGOs. This scheme was administered by the prefectural government which coopted PENCE at a later phase to supervise and follow-up progress in the field. The credit in kind consisted of one male and four female small ruminants for a family. The total number of recipients was 570 families. The recipient was expected to repay in kind the same number of animals after reconstituting a basic stock. Project officials were unable to give figures on repayment or default but said that many recipients of the first round did repay, and the scheme was extended to more people.

Several factors seem to have undermined the continuity of the scheme. The prefecture was not the appropriate level of authority to administer it. The project was not actively involved. The GMPs were not utilized as the points of credit distribution and supervision. The poorest recipients sold the animals to meet immediate subsistence needs and defaulted as a result. In some cases the animals died. The experience showed that five small ruminants were too small a unit as a starting point for reconstitution. Some sources put the minimum at twenty animals. The demographic status of the family and its preferences with regard to species composition should be considered in determining the size and composition of the stock provided to reconstitute the herd.

Services

Animal health. The six CPs are the main suppliers of government and project services. Their establishment has brought health care services, literacy and training closer to the intended beneficiaries. They have also made direct communication between project personnel and the pastoralists easier. Animal health is of primary concern and the project has achieved good results in basic animal health. The veterinary personnel in the CPs are responsible for annual vaccination campaigns and the treatment of more serious animal ailments. Each center has a small veterinary clinic with a veterinary assistant. Drugs can be purchased at the CPs and the GVC cooperative shops, and from some of the veterinary assistants in the GMPs. Pastoralists complained that drug prices were too high. The project officials explained that pricing was in accordance with the national policy of making the beneficiaries pay a reasonable price for the services they receive. In 1985, the project started training veterinary assistants at the GMP level and by the end of 1988 a total of 81 had been trained. The training program is to be resumed.

Human health. Since 1985, PENCE has paid greater attention to human health. Each CP has a small clinic and a nurse with a small stock of basic drugs. The CPs have trained several midwives and health assistants at the GMP level. Some of the GMPs have a first aid kit. The supply of new medicine can be slow.

Literacy. The pastoral zone is not covered by national literacy campaigns. Literacy programs in Tamasheq, Arabic, and Toubou at the CPs began in 1985-86. Attendance is very low; for example at the Tejira CP, only twenty people have attended literacy classes in the last four years. Illiteracy is a major constraint to PO development and at the present pace the literacy program is not going to make a dent in the foreseeable future. There is also the likelihood of the program ending if the French funding stops. The need to identify the bottle-necks preventing wider participation and to intensify the approach to literacy cannot be over-emphasized. The scope of the literacy program has to be substantially expanded with a larger number of teachers and a wider dispersion of literacy centers to induce wider participation. This challenge cannot be successfully tackled unless the government extends the national literacy campaign to the pastoral zone and supports the project's short-term programs.

Leadership and management skills

As the GMPs are formed according to traditional tribal affinities, they are dominated by traditional chiefs and their families. In this respect, observations in the other countries are fully valid for Niger as well (see, for example, the Mali case). The extremely low level of literacy in the official language, French, among GMP leaders is a strong barrier to institutional progress. The conduct of official correspondence in French seems highly impractical from the point of view of making the GMPs work better. The communication problem (and hence many misunderstandings and delays) could be considerably reduced if the CP could communicate with the GMP in the local languages. The lack of literacy in French among GMP leaders has made them dependent on the field staff of the project on practically all administrative matters.

The GMP committees need training in well management and ways to increase revenues, in environmental protection, and in basic accounting and financial management. This training has to be conducted in the local languages. The challenge facing the project is to identify the few who are literate enough in their own languages to follow such training and motivate them to learn these skills.

The field staff in the Nigerien project appear to be more engaged in PO development than their counterparts in the other countries. They are indeed playing leadership roles. This has helped to create and sustain momentum in the formation and functioning of GMPs. However, in the absence of more intensive literacy and training, permanent dependence of the committees on the field staff could result, defeating the end aim of institution building.

Economic viability

The PO development process in Niger is still in its very early stages, with only about five years of uninterrupted evolution. It is almost totally dependent on external financing. A withdrawal of financial support would bring the whole process to an abrupt end. However, there is potential for the GMPs to become financially more self-supporting especially those with their own water points. They have yet to tap the revenue-generating potential of the GMP wells. GMPs located far away from the CP and the GVC could set up their own sales points for drugs and food items, and earn profits. They could introduce more regular membership fees. These prospects are dependent on development management skills which are constrained by low literacy and inadequate resources.

Time, money, and professional skills are needed to make the Nigerien plan work. The most immediate needs in the field are: (a) more rapid and extensive mobilization of the pastoralists into GMPs; (b) steps to increase the money-making abilities of GMPs; (c) literacy and leadership training; (d) completion of the formation of the GVCs and development of plans for rangeland and tree management; (e) establishment of cooperative shops in all the GVCs; (f) a credit scheme for herd reconstitution at the GMP level and (g) sustaining and expanding the services at the CP.

Other issues should be addressed concurrently. The government has yet to implement the long-awaited tenurial reforms and commit itself more seriously to pastoral development. The Livestock Department did not display the same interest in PO development as it did in animal health campaigns. As observed in a project document, "There was no permanent entity at the central government level fully acquainted with and open-minded on pastoral questions." There were problems regarding the release of counterpart funds and acceptance of responsibility for recurrent costs on completion of the project period.

With such a record of government-project relations, reservations about the future of pastoral institution building in the project area may be justified. But the activities initiated by the project are worth supporting, and if the project were to be terminated, appropriate alternatives should be adopted in time to prevent disruption.

Senegal

Several factors specific to the area made the formation of pastoral organizations easier in Senegal than in other countries in the region. The population is largely agro-pastoralist, more settled, with livestock and human movements taking place within a limited area. The climatic conditions of relatively high and regular rainfall, although below long-term average in the implementation period, are more favorable, and the water table higher at about 40 to 50 meters. Because there is no evidence of over-stocking, the project did not have to address the controversial issue of de-stocking among members.

Under review are two development projects in Eastern Senegal involving the livestock sector. The Senegal Livestock Development Project (1976-80) is referred to as Phase I, and the livestock component of the Eastern Senegal Rural Development Project (1983-90) as Phase II. A Phase III will pick up a limited part of the two first phases under a National Program for Integrated Natural Resource Management (PICOGERNA).

The objectives of Phase I were to assist 30,000 livestock owners to increase their incomes by developing and operating a grazing scheme and making livestock inputs readily available, and to improve the animal health service. Phase II was to consolidate the achievements of Phase I by further improvements in animal health, input and extension service, credit, implementation of the grazing plans, and functional literacy.

The target population of the project is the 70,000 agro-pastoralists within an area of 14,000 square kilometers in the PDESO zone north of the Dakar-Tambacounda road. The project falls in the Sudano-Guinean zone with rainfall variation between 700 mm in the north and 1400 mm in the south. About 60 percent of target population are Peul, the rest Wolof and Mandingo. The people are agro-pastoralist, settled in permanent villages. Short-range transhumance by young men for two or three months of the year to distant water points and *mares* is practiced. The traditional territorial organizations are based on lineage and caste, but were not operating very efficiently before the project interventions (Bromley and Cernea 1989).

Despite losses during droughts and enhanced off-take, livestock populations have increased constantly since the start of the project to 136,000 cattle and 140,000 goats and sheep. The livestock density is about 7 TLU per sq. km, well below carrying capacity (Centre Suivi Ecolologique, CSU 1990). Local overgrazing and land-use conflicts between livestock and cultivation were becoming increasingly common in the more densely populated areas in the drought years prior to the project start. Land-use conflicts arose particularly where transhumant pastoralists entered the area from northern Senegal and Mauritania. Crop land covers about 4 percent of the area and is expanding fast (Le Grand 1988). Integration of livestock with crop cultivation, such as collection of manure and use of animal traction, is increasing, but is still at a modest level. Chemical fertilizers are little used, for economic reasons. Depletion of soil nutrients due to shorter fallow periods in the agro-pastoral areas is an issue which has not been addressed. Deforestation is a major environmental problem. Bush fires are frequent.

The appraisal mission of Phase I, which included a sociologist, rejected a proposal to establish fattening ranches, and instead recommended conversion of the entire area from open access to a common property regime managed by pastoralists, to be organized into pastoral grazing units (Bromley and Cernea 1989).

PO formation

By 1980, 53 pastoral units (PUs) were established, with elected management committees (MCs) (*Comités de Gestion*). The PUs are groups of pastoralists living in villages located in the same area and using the same rangeland. The 60 PUs now established are all legally approved as economic organizations called *Groupements d'Intérêt Economique* (GIEs). The GIEs are recognized by two national laws passed in 1984 and 1985 (Loi No. 84-37 and Loi No. 85-40).

The boards of the GIEs are elected at general assemblies in which village delegates participate. The boards enter into an agreement *(Protocol d'Accord)* with the project management (PDESO), signed also by the *Sous-Préfet* and the Presidents of the Rural Councils (RCs) concerned. The RCs are the basic unit of local government.

The main functions of the GIEs are to organize and educate their members, encourage rational use of agricultural and pastoral areas, facilitate livestock development and provide guarantees for credit taken by members. The average size of a PU/GIE is 1,200 people. The average GIE territory is 24,000 square kilometers. The GIEs supervise the establishment of management committees at village level, which is the basic unit of the PO system.

About 50 percent of the potential members of a GIE in a given locality are actually members (Le Grand 1988), providing a relatively strong membership base for further development. Board members are elected from villages representing different geographical zones. Each GIE has about 50 heads-of-household members, providing a manageable group for decisionmaking.

Board members come from the nobility, which constitutes about 70 percent of the population. The society is stratified in a caste system, and the 20 percent who are slaves are without influence in decisionmaking (Annual Report 1988). There are no female office-bearers in the GIEs, although women exert limited pressure on the village PO and GIE decisionmaking through women's groups. There are fewer than ten women's groups in the whole project area; women are more active participants in village level meetings than in GIE meetings.

Younger educated men are replacing traditional leaders in many of the GIEs, but the younger leaders still consult the elders in important decisions. The participation of the elders in the decisionmaking lends authority to GIE boards ensuring that decisions are followed-up at the village level.

The GIEs have improved the management of the rangeland and reduced the frequency of resource-use conflicts both within and between pastoral communities. Many of them made progress towards economic viability, but the overall performance is uneven. The relative success of the project in agro-pastoral institution building is to a large extent due to work done at the appraisal stage, when socio-economic data on local institutions and resource use were used to shape project formulation. The process of data gathering also opened communication channels between the staff and the participants. The project leadership and the key technical personnel were competent and hard-working. Staff-continuity was good in Phase I but not in Phase II. Supervision by the World Bank was good. During Phase I the implementing agency, SODIFITEX, was able to pre-finance project expenditures at a time when government counterpart funds were lacking.

These factors combined with the area-specific advantages mentioned earlier, contributed to the general above-average performance of the project in relation to the disappointing record of livestock projects in Sub-Saharan Africa (World Bank Experience 1965-86, World Bank 1988).

Food security

Despite some loss of animals during the droughts and some dispossession of animals, the food security situation, according to project staff, is better now than before the project intervention. In general livestock and agricultural production have increased at the household level.

Resource security

The agreements with the government provide the GIE with certain rights to use the land and water resources, and certain obligations regarding range management, but not tenure or usufruct right in a legal sense.

The lack of water is a main constraint to development. The project constructed 111 wells and rehabilitated 20 water points. Public water boreholes are provided by the Department of Water. The project has not, however, been able to develop village-level responsibility for the management of the wells and water points, which are still maintained by the project and considered project or government property. Only around a few public boreholes with pumps have borehole management committees been established to collect water fees, pay a trained borehole technician, and maintain the water pump. These committees receive little training and support and their performance is very uneven.

Grazing management. Central to the project approach was the grazing management scheme, which started well. Competent project staff were recruited early, and management plans were thoroughly discussed with the PU management committees. By 1984 almost all the PUs had developed grazing management plans including both general rules for range management and specific measures for each locality. Implementation of the plans led to more rational use of pasture, protection of previously overgrazed areas, better organization of bush fire control, and better resolution of local resource-use conflicts. Local awareness of environmental conflicts increased.

The project management has not, however, supervised the implementation of the grazing plans over the last few years. Many of the plans are now outdated, and the GIEs do not have the competence to revise the plans on their own.

They may also lack the necessary motivation to do so, since the pastoralists do not regard overgrazing as a major constraint to livestock development in the area. A recent survey confirms that overgrazing is not widespread, but is a localized problem in the PDESO zone. According to CSE, large areas of the PDESO zone remain underutilized because of to understocking and non-availability of water (CSE 1990). This is in contrast to the project preparation documents, which stressed that overgrazing was a major problem in the project area. The apparent improvement in grazing conditions over the last few years can probably be explained by better rains, but some local improvement in rangeland management during the project implementation may have contributed.

Bush fires. About 50 percent of the rangeland burns every year, which is destructive for pasture availability in the dry season. Phase I included construction of 2,400 km of firebreaks, but only 900 km were made because of delays and because the Forestry Department did not have the resources to maintain the system. The firebreaks are now overgrown with vegetation and are no longer effective. The establishment of bush fire control committees at the village level has increased awareness of the need to control fires. Fires are less frequent than before, but practical actions against bush fires are limited to some early burning of circles in the near surroundings of the villages. The pastoralists claim that they lack labor and equipment such as hand pumps, fire-bats, and axes to carry out efficient fire fighting and firebreak maintenance.

Deforestation is a major problem caused by expansion in cultivation, cutting for charcoal and fuelwood, and improper exploitation of gum arabic. Management of the natural forest has not been a preoccupation of the project. Reforestation through village plantations has been limited to about 450 square kilometers, which is insignificant compared to the rate of deforestation. The GIEs could be given a role in the management of natural forests, if they were authorized to collect fees for permits to exploit the forest. At present there is no effective control on tree-cutting because the Forestry Department does not have the resources to manage the forests properly.

The pastoralists have not increased the proportion of small ruminants or camels in their herds, as a survival strategy for drought years. Cattle still represent 70 to 80 percent of the total stock in TLU (CSE 1990).

Herd ownership

The share of herds owned by urban dwellers is said by project staff and pastoralists to be increasing, but the pastoralists did not regard this as controversial.

Services

Animal health. This main service provided by the project is highly appreciated by the pastoralists. The vaccination campaign is the most important aspect. All major animal diseases are under control. A main reason for the pastoralists to join the GIEs is the access which membership gives to the animal health services, in particular to the GIE veterinary drug stores. About 50 of the GIEs have been granted a revolving fund of 200,000 FCFA to establish drug stores. The drugs are bought in Tambacounda and sold at a higher price by the GIE. The profits are used to renew stocks and pay the auxiliaries, who normally run the stores. Reimbursement of the revolving fund has varied from 65 to 90 percent. About 15 of the GIEs are now, after three or four years, able to manage their drug stores properly.

Some 300 pastoralists were selected from the literacy program to undergo further training in animal husbandry, resource management, and literacy training to form a cadre of young animal health and literacy extension agents to serve their own communities. Sound and commendable in concept, the experiment is not yet finalized. About half of those trained have stopped functioning, a main problem being lack of payment, which is a responsibility of the GIEs.

Literacy. Functional literacy was stressed as a precondition for producer participation in the project and the management of the POs under the preparation of both Phase I and Phase II. From its start in 1979, almost 9,000 people (more than 10 percent of the population) have been through the literacy program. The program has covered 300 villages out of 430 (70 percent). Women's participation was low, about 10 percent; the drop-out rate was 30 percent. Given the various constraints to conducting a literacy program, the overall achievement appears remarkable in a region where literacy was almost zero.

Marketing. The livestock market is operated by a complex system of private traders and intermediaries, and is relatively efficient, but exploits the pastoralists. An attempt by the project to assist the POs in organizing marketing failed because of competition from the traditional dealers. A more limited effort by the project to assist a few pastoralists in the marketing of stall-fed animals in Dakar was, however, carried out successfully.

Leadership and management training

A recent survey among 51 of the GIEs revealed a very low level of literacy among the key GIE office-holders. Only about 30 percent of the presidents and vice-presidents were considered literate, 60 percent of the secretaries, 27 percent of the treasurers and 20 percent of the accountants. It is inconceivable how an illiterate person could function as a bookkeeper or treasurer or secretary. This situation raises the question of the project's priority and resource allocation for literacy and training. A training program for Board members at GIE and village levels should have been given higher priority.

Ethnic factors

The Wolof and Mandingo have been more efficient in organizing their GIEs and their economic activities than the Peul. Their traditional organizations are stricter and stronger, particularly above village level, their average literacy level higher, and their leaders have more power and influence in matters of common concern than is the case among the Peul.

Economic viability

The new POs have been under operation for about ten years, five years as management committees for PUs and five years as GIEs. An evaluation of the GIEs in 1987-88 indicates that 24 out of 58 GIEs were able to keep proper records over production inputs, handle the distribution of inputs and collect money for repayment of credit. None of the GIEs had reached the level of autonomous economic institutions. The future of the GIEs as independent viable institutions depends on their ability to improve their economic foundation. More systematic collection of membership fees and more efficient operation of the drug stores can provide higher revenues, but the main opportunities to improve the revenues lie in livestock activities such as fattening and milk units financed through credit. Efforts should be made to help the GIEs to improve the organization of livestock marketing. Through group sales of animals, members could negotiate better prices with private dealers.

The project was completed in 1990 and the future support for the GIEs depends on the direction of the Phase III follow-up program (PICOGERNA). Several problems may affect the sustainability of the GIEs: (a) GIEs do not have the necessary minimum technical knowledge to revise the grazing plans, and the capacity of the present project to assist is limited. (b) The GIEs have not been encouraged to take responsibility for water management, and the government has not provided for the conversion of public wells into communal wells managed by local committees. (c) The village level institutions such as chiefs, religious chiefs, and village meetings in these settled agro-pastoral societies have major influence on land use, transhumance and mobilization for NRM, and are in reality the primary units of the POs. The project has so far focused on the formation of GIEs at a higher level at the expense of support to and training of management committees and traditional leaders at the village level. (d) The introduction of new NRM activities, such as rehabilitation of firebreaks and tree planting, has not been based on adequate local participation. (e) The POs are still not economically viable and face problems in generating revenues for remuneration of the pastoral agents, whose roles are crucial.

The PICOGERNA is intended to maintain only some of the project activities and to support only one third of the existing GIEs. The GIEs not eligible for further support may collapse. Continued government support to the GIEs in the form of credit and extension and training will be necessary for some years. This view is supported by a recent assessment of twelve of the best-functioning GIEs (Le - Grand, 1988).

4. *A Comparative Analysis of the Country Experiences*

The institution building processes reviewed show that the governments concerned have recognized the importance of developing local capacities and involving the people in resource management, and with the support of the World Bank, have taken certain steps toward that end. The projects have contributed to the growing awareness among pastoralists of environmental problems. But shortcomings in policy, project organization, and management are evident.

Among the four projects under review, pastoral institution building received the lowest priority in Mali. In the other three countries, some steps were taken toward creating an enabling environment for POs, although they conceptualized POs in their own ways. The Nigerien project developed a three-tier model which differentiates between water point management (GMP) and range management (GVC) levels while the apex body, CP, provides the main services. Its major practical achievement regarding NRM so far is the conversion of public wells into GMP wells. It has not reached the stage of spatial demarcation and range management, but adopted food security and essential services as rallying points for POs after the 1983-84 drought.

The Senegalese project progressed in the direction of demarcating pastoral units, setting-up GIEs, and providing grazing rights with well-defined obligations. It has designed grazing schemes while neglecting the issue of water rights and water point management. The Mauritanian project has demarcated the spatial boundaries for the POs, but has not adequately focused on water management, and the village level as the basic unit. All three have paid attention to training local level personnel to varying degrees.

However, there are constraints of financial and professional resources as well as major government and project failures in all four countries. One of the most evident manifestations of these shortcomings is the continued dominance of the top-down character of PO formation. The governments and the projects have not been able to turn the top-down initiative for PO development into a bottom-up process of mobilization. This situation is a product of unresolved issues.

Local Priorities vs. Project Objectives

Sometimes projects are not supported by their intended beneficiaries because the objectives of the project do not coincide with the priorities of the beneficiaries. Certainly, there are gaps between the priorities of the livestock projects and those of the pastoralists. A project intervention in the pastoral areas raises the expectations of the intended beneficiaries. The expectations are not necessarily based on the objectives of the project, but on the more deeply felt basic needs of the people. When a project goes to an area which lacks basic infrastructure and services, the people expect the project to satisfy the needs hitherto neglected by the state. For example, pastoralists in an area without basic health services do not see any logic in giving animal health a higher priority than human health. But it appears logical to the designers of a livestock development project to give higher priority to animal health and identify human health as a topic for the state's health department or for other projects specifically concerned with it. Closer collaboration between the project and the essential services of the government is obviously needed, but not possible where these essential services such as health and education do not exist. The consequence is that weakness and failure of the government are reflected as weakness and failure of the project.

Common Problems

Food security and drought contingency plans

There is a specific link between pastoral institution building and food security in the Sahel. When drought is protracted, pastoralists migrate in search of food, pasture and water, and may end up in distant places for periods as long as one to five years before returning to their "base" areas. Often they settle around permanent water points or near centers where food aid and animal and human health services are available.

An immediate consequence of this dispersal of intended beneficiaries is the disruption of the institution building process itself. None of the four projects reviewed had paid adequate attention to the probability of a drought occurring during the project period. Hence, no systematic contingency plans were made to minimize displacement and dispersion of affected pastoralists. The 1983-84 drought led to large-scale animal losses and migration of pastoralists in Mali, Niger and Mauritania.

An important lesson is that food security is not only a good rallying point for PO formation, but drought contingency plans, including supplementary animal feed stocks, emergency assistance in animal marketing, and credit for regeneration of herds should be treated as essential components of pastoral development projects if major discontinuities with their consequences for NRM are to be avoided. Only the Nigerien project has taken the lesson seriously after the drought and adopted food security as a key factor in its PO development effort. There are, however, problems of finding the financial and the managerial resources for the start-up and efficient functioning of cooperative shops supplying provisions to PO members.

Identification of project beneficiaries

Another defect common to all the projects is the lack of a clear and comprehensive demarcation of the intended beneficiaries. Project documents mention population figures in the project areas without adequate descriptions of the socio-cultural conditions and institutions of resource management. All such populations are internally differentiated in terms of herd ownership and access to natural resources. The growth of absentee herd ownership has considerably altered the traditional social structures of pastoral communities. There is a growing population of paid-herders or pastoral laborers whose most immediate need may be better wages and terms of employment or the opportunity to become herd owners again. The projects had no explicit stand on the role of women. Project planning seems to have taken place as if these elements of the population did not exist or if they did, had no major implications for pastoral institution building. Yet they are of direct relevance to PO development. The role of women is discussed more fully in a separate chapter.

Design of grazing schemes and NRM activities

Only the Senegalese project has developed grazing plans for the POs based on formalized agreements between the POs and the government. These agreements include obligations on behalf of the POs to follow certain rangeland management principles. While these plans seem technically sound, they appear to be beyond the present capacities of POs to implement and revise without closer and more active involvement of the project staff.

Financial allocations

The financial, professional, and logistical resources allocated to pastoral institution building remained low and inadequate in all the projects. Only in the Mauritanian and the Senegalese projects had more than 10 percent of the total budget been allocated to PO formation and development.

Membership criteria and spatial delineation

Little attention has been paid to the distinction between membership in a local cohesive traditional group and membership in the PO based on it. Only in Senegal and Mauritania have PO boundaries been clearly demarcated, using a criterion combining residence and kinship affinity. The spatial delineation remains incomplete in Mali and Niger, adding to the problems of defining a clear concept of membership to distinguish members from non-members. In none of the countries have the POs been able to establish formal requirements such as fixed membership fees. Within the PO boundaries members and non-members of state-sponsored POs cannot easily be distinguished. In general, non-members are provided with the same services and given the same privileges as members if they reside in the same area. Hence, people do not always see the point of being a PO member. This is an obvious constraint on membership mobilization and ways must be found to overcome it.

Membership criteria should normally be based on one or more of the following factors: residence in a particular area and use of common water points on rangeland, kinship, ethnic and other affinities, payment of membership fees granting special concessions to members in charges for and access to water and services. The criteria to be used would vary depending on the proposed functions of the POs and the local environmental and social conditions. A criterion based exclusively on residence would, for example, not be suitable in the more arid and nomadic areas in Niger, Mali, and Mauritania.

Competence and training of PO leadership

The competence and efficiency of the PO leadership are crucial for successful progress in the work of POs. The PO leaders are mostly recruited from the traditional chiefs and their relatives. Inevitable in the early phases, this situation may not be undesirable if the leaders are competent and willing to meet the new organizational challenges and the needs of the pastoralists. In several cases younger and more literate men have replaced the traditional leaders as secretaries and accountants. While this is a positive development, it also reflects the fact that many of the PO leaders are illiterate and lack the necessary skills to perform the new tasks required of them. The PO leaders are, for example, weak in economic management, accounting and new technologies for NRM. They may also lack competence to organize NRM at village or PO levels. Only in Mauritania was there a powerful promotion of the pastoral interests through the PO leaders at the national level. Although there is an obvious need for management training, none of the projects has an extensive and sustained training program for the PO leaders.

The Senegalese project is the only one with a substantial literacy training component. The leadership tasks in the new POs have made literacy an indispensable prerequisite for pastoral institution building. A group without at least a few men and women who are literate in the official language faces great problems in furthering its cause. Since most pastoral areas are not covered by national literacy programs, literacy has to be an important high priority component of a project with PO-building as an objective. At the same time, there should be arrangements with the national literacy program and educational system to ensure continuity of the program started by the project after the project's completion. However, literacy is a necessary but not a sufficient precondition for successful PO development. In the absence of adequate economic prospects and basic security in the form of herd ownership, the more literate young may be more easily induced to migrate to urban centers in search of paid employment. Only if basic economic security is assured, are the more literate young more likely to stay and seek leadership positions in POs.

Training of pastoral agents

Pastoral agents play an important role in motivating and training pastoralists and in providing extension and other services. The training of pastoral agents from the local population has been most impressive in Senegal and Niger. In Mali this work has not been given priority. The projects in Senegal and Niger have not, however, been able to develop satisfactory arrangements at the PO level to remunerate the agents who have to forego income from herding to devote time to extension work. This failure has demotivated many agents.

Absentee herd ownership

Absentee herd ownership and paid herding increased dramatically during and after the droughts. In Mali local researchers indicated that as much as 80 percent of the herds might be owned by non-pastoralists, although these figures are difficult to verify and should be treated with caution. Only in Niger did the project attempt to address the problem of dispossession of animals by providing credit for reconstitution of the herds, even in a small way.

There seems to be a lack of awareness on the part of the governments and the donors (including the World Bank) of the consequences of the growing absentee herd ownership for pastoral institution building and NRM. This is a difficult and controversial policy issue in all the countries. The problems of absentee herd ownership are most visible in Mali, and have a negative effect on the management of the resources in the Niger delta. Absentee ownership implies a separation between herd ownership and management that is not conducive to livestock enterprise development, pastoral institution building, or NRM. The problem must be addressed at the policy level since it involves issues such as price, tax policies, and investment options. Higher taxes and the lack of investment alternatives more profitable than livestock, are among the main reasons for transfer of investible surpluses to the livestock sector in the form of absentee herd ownership.

Animal health services - a benefit

In all the projects except Mali, revolving funds for veterinary drug stores have been introduced to the POs. In Senegal, about half the POs are now able to keep proper record of stocks, handle the distribution of drugs, and collect money for repayment of the credit. But lack of skills in economics and book-keeping is a major problem for the management of the stores and the revolving funds.

Overall, the animal health services have been the most important benefit provided by the projects. Most of the livestock is now vaccinated annually and the main animal diseases are under control. The veterinary services have played a major role in the regeneration of herds. The services are highly appreciated by the pastoralists, and have helped build confidence. Logistical problems such as lack of transport, fuel, long distances and bad roads make the services a costly exercise for the governments, raising the need for privatization. Given the inefficiencies of the existing government-controlled systems for importation, distribution, and sale of veterinary drugs, the initiatives for privatization in the projects are sound. The experience from various countries shows that the establishment of private veterinary pharmacies takes time, whether established on a cooperative basis by POs or by private individuals. Veterinarians who wish to establish private practices are also faced with problems of raising the initial capital, and uncertainty of future income.

Overall, the process of privatization has often been slower than anticipated. A declared policy of privatization can easily become an excuse for the governments to let the present public service deteriorate in the initial phases of a privatization process. Even under full privatization the governments may find it necessary to provide some subsidies for animal health services in the more remote areas, where the income base for veterinarians and veterinary drug stores would be low.

Credit

In general, pastoralists and POs are not seen as creditworthy by rural and national development banks in the four countries. As a result the availability of institutional credit for pastoralists and POs is very low in all projects. The repayment rate for the credit provided by the projects has been analyzed only in Senegal, where it varied between 60 and 90 percent. Credit facilities are necessary if POs are to find their own ways to attain economic viability. This calls for innovative schemes which are not likely to emerge in the current credit policy environment.

Animal marketing

Assistance in animal marketing was not meant to be a major project activity. A few marketing centers have been constructed by the projects, and studies of animal marketing have been financed. One attempt by the project in Senegal to provide direct assistance for POs in cattle sales in Dakar failed because of competition from the traditional traders, indicating that direct interventions may not be fruitful. However, the bargaining position of livestock owners is weak because they are almost entirely dependent on traders for market information, and they are not organized to collectively promote their interest in livestock market transactions. Even though the projects could have played a role in meeting these needs, they were not prepared to do so.

Economic viability of POs and external dependence

There are little data available at the project level on the socio-economic and financial performance of the POs. There have not been systematic efforts to monitor these aspects of PO development in any of the projects. It appeared that all four projects lacked a functioning monitoring and evaluation system covering the economic state of the POs they had set up and formalized. The standard explanation given by officials for this deficiency was that the POs were not yet capable of collecting and providing the necessary information.

From the limited information gathered, and from some studies on the Senegalese project, POs in Senegal appear to have performed better than those in the other countries. But most of the POs are still not economically sustainable, and their viability generally depends on further external support from the government or other donors. They are unable even to generate adequate funds to satisfactorily remunerate their own pastoral agents. This situation is a product of shortcomings at different levels. At the PO level, it is a reflection of the lack of leadership to identify revenue-generating activities and organize them efficiently. But this task cannot be satisfactorily accomplished without active support from the project in the form of professional inputs including training in the initial stages.

Participation of sociologists and environmental experts

The governments and donors have not sufficiently appreciated the particular requirements of the pastoral institution building and NRM programs for the active involvement of sociologists and environmental experts in planning and implementation. Such experts are indispensable for a better understanding of the social structures and dynamics of pastoral communities and local priorities for NRM. The Senegalese and Mauritanian projects did, however, enjoy a better input of such resources than the Malian project.

Staff competence and motivation

The composition of project staff in terms of professional skills and gender is another area of concern. The implementing agencies have been predominantly staffed with veterinary personnel, and women are conspicuously absent in technical positions. Social scientists, competent sociologists and institutional economists in particular, are too few on the project staff. In the Malian project, there are two sociologists at the head office. One of them, a woman, is responsible for women's cooperatives. The other heads the PO division and appears to be occupied mostly with administrative matters at the project head office in Mopti. There seems to be no effective linkage between the activities of PO and the women's cooperative divisions. There are no personnel at the field level with specialized competence in rural cooperation, NRM and PO development. All 212 field staff are veterinary personnel with limited or no skills in these activities. They have, no doubt, performed their veterinary tasks well.

The Nigerien project engaged two local sociologists who were able to make a significant contribution toward a better understanding of the sociological aspects and the mobility patterns of the different pastoral communities. It was also apparent that the field personnel in Niger had a reasonable orientation on the problem of GMP formation and mobilization of the people. Most of the 34 field staff have been trained in animal health. Each Pastoral Center has an *animateur* responsible for the formation of GMPs. Most field staff in the Nigerien project are on temporary employment contracts which expired in June 1991. At present their salaries are being paid from funds granted by the French Government. If their services are discontinued after June 1991 the future progress of the GMPs will be severely handicapped.

The Mauritanian project has one sociologist assisted by two persons. The team is based at the project head office in Nouakchott and travels through the project area of 130,000 sq. km. organizing POs. Even though the sociologist and the staff are highly dedicated, the vastness of the project area and the poor infrastructure make their task extremely arduous. The team is assisted in the field by the veterinary personnel of the project. There are no field level *animateurs* yet, but recently the project started to post young extension officers to serve each of the POs.

The Senegalese project had a sociologist for a few years. At present there is one extension and training officer with experience in PO formation, and one resource planner at Tambacounda with competence in physical planning. There are *animateurs* working with most of the POs.

Institutional competence building

All projects have faced serious implementation problems and delays which can be related to administrative and organizational deficiencies in the implementing agencies. Particular problems are weak economic planning and financial management, budgeting, accounting, and auditing. There was a lack of competence in PO formation and NRM, both in relation to technical and managerial skills. These weakness have often had negative effects on the field services in PO formation and training. The reasons for these institutional weakness are partly to be found in the external political and institutional environment in which the agencies operate. But there are also important factors internal to the agencies.

The projects, including the PO formation and NRM components, are relatively complex integrated exercises which put particular demands on the competence and capacity of the implementing agency. The build-up of sociological and environmental capacity in the implementing agency requires long-term assistance. These agencies have, however, received some strengthening through Technical Assistance (TA) support. Nevertheless, short-term technical assistance has proved to be of dubious value. Lack of continuity in technical assistance is a well-known problem. The use of a visiting sociologist from an established institution has proven effective in the case of Mauritania. But TA costs are high, foreign experts are controversial in executive roles, and high reliance on them makes it difficult to transfer management responsibility to national staff when they leave. This raises the need for institution building at the national and project levels.

In all projects, there has been a lack of systematic institutional approach to human resources development within the implementing agencies. Efforts to strengthen the implementing agencies have often focused on upgrading the skills of individual staff members without a proper policy of institutional competence-building.

Project Termination

None of the projects had a fully organized plan for phasing-out project components to government departments. Even though the projects have existed for many years, their termination may seem abrupt because of the lack of planning. The problem is already evident in Niger where the project has been formally terminated without adequate arrangements for the pastoral institution building component to continue. There is great uncertainty about the future of this and other project components. An immediate consequence of this uncertainty is the demoralization of the field staff employed by the project. Their departure from the project could cause severe disruption to PO development. The PO component of the Senegalese project is faced with similar uncertainties. The Malian project's already weak PO component is also likely to be affected as the project terminates. In all these cases, the governments have no comprehensive plans for the continuing development of POs.

Political Commitment and Land and Water Rights

Two of the most important policy-level issues are the degree of political commitment and the adequacy of existing tenurial institutions.

In all the four countries, there was some form of explicit governmental approval and policy commitment to PO building. The actual steps taken by governments, in terms of policy, institutional reforms, and public investment, are more important than the semantics of their commitment. Judging from the project areas, pastoral development has tended to receive lower priority than agricultural development (fishery development in the case of Mauritania). In general, the Nigerien, Mauritanian and Senegalese governments have shown greater concern to promote pastoral institution building than their Malian counterpart. Institutional reforms to put POs on a sound legal footing and to grant tenurial rights are inadequate to varying degrees in all cases. The governments' progress in institutional reforms are lagging behind the pastoralists' needs for such reforms by several years. The existing land laws are more favorable to agriculturalists than pastoralists in terms of tenurial security.

National literacy programs are inadequate in Mauritania, Mali, and Senegal, and non-existent in Niger in the project areas. This implies that the literacy programs initiated by the projects may not be sustained and expanded or may come to an abrupt end as the projects conclude. The same may be said about human health facilities for most parts of the project areas. Governmental administrative structures appear to be weak in the project areas in all four countries. The low project allocations coupled with the weak or non-existent governmental backing for activities like literacy, NRM, and public health have hampered PO formation and development. The flow of funds to the projects has been irregular and often inadequate, putting severe strain on day-to-day operations, for example on field services. Availability of government counterpart funds has been a problem in all the projects.

Water and land rights remain subjects in which conflicts and uncertainties abound because the contradictions between different property regimes and land-use policies have adverse effects on pastoralism. In the colonial period, state property became a dominant form and continues to be, giving the state the right to allocate lands for uses it deems best. Agricultural expansion has meant an expansion of private ownership. This is a necessary development. However, when it goes on without corresponding institutional changes to promote sustainable pastoralism, intersectoral conflicts and environmental degradation tend to increase.

In practice, state-owned grazing land and water points are open access resources for which nobody feels responsible. They are everybody's property and hence nobody's property. This has put the question of reconstituting viable commons on the agenda of tenurial reform, but policy action seems to be slow. While shari'a—the Islamic code—is cited by pastoralists and officials as the customary law that guides usufruct rights to rangeland and water resources, it is also conceded by the same sources that traditionally defensible rights are being undermined or denied by the officially sponsored or promoted or condoned new land-use systems which are based on private ownership.

In the complex arena of conflicts between the traditional shari'a and the pre-Islamic customs that still endure on one side, and modern property laws on the other, interpretations of rights vary, leaving the final word to the state's judiciary. According to the shari'a, usufruct or private ownership of land may be granted to a user who has "developed" the land. The dominant interpretation is that pastoral land-use is not an activity that develops the land. This apparent legal barrier may become a real barrier to effective implementation of the policy of ecological restoration and sustainable natural resource management. Pastoralists would prefer to have legally defensible communal usufruct or priority rights to their grazing lands before they invest in water points and range improvement and management, and thereby "develop" the land.

Land and water rights in the four countries are discussed more fully in the Annex.

Lessons from the Projects

The Senegalese project progressed best toward fulfilling some of the basic conditions for rangeland management. The factors specific to Senegal were more conducive to success. However, certain lessons from the Senegalese project are relevant to pastoral institution building in general. These pertain to project planning and governmental action.

- Project planning in Senegal was more systematically undertaken and was based on a relatively sound knowledge of the local socio-economic and environmental conditions.
- The project area was declared a pilot zone. The POs component was understood to be a long-term activity involving definition of pastoral units, planning of grazing schemes, and training of pastoral agents from the target groups.
- The POs rights to land were legally recognized early in the implementation period.
- Project staff, assisted by external experts, took an active interest in spatial demarcation and developing grazing schemes.
- As the competence of the POs improved, they were legally recognized as economic entities and granted access to revolving funds for veterinary pharmacies and income-generating activities.
- The project trained several pastoral agents for each PO in NRM, animal health, and production.
- The implementing agency functioned efficiently because of competent and motivated

staff. It was able to mobilize funds when transfer of government funds was unduly delayed-evidence of the commitment of the project leadership to expedite implementation.

• The implementing agency was located at the center of the project area and was delegated sufficient authority to take important decisions and reach formal agreements with POs on grazing rights and obligations.

• The project was able to achieve 10 percent literacy in the area through its own programs.

• The project's allocations for the POs component were relatively higher than those of the other projects—more than 10 percent as against less than 5 percent in Niger and Mali.

These factors imply reasonable governmental backing for PO formation and a satisfactory working relationship with the government. But the Senegalese project would have fared even better if water rights had been included in the grazing agreement. There are also signs that the project's progress is suffering due to the dropping-out of pastoral agents and the changes taking place in resource allocation under the new project. These developments show that the POs have not yet become self-sustaining and the gains of the past may be lost if external technical support is not provided for a further period.

The Mauritanian project showed some positive results in a relatively short period of two years mainly attributable to:

• A well-designed approach implemented by a competent and motivated project team with support from the government. The team was headed by a local sociologist familiar with local conditions. An expatriate sociologist with a good knowledge of the Mauritanian society participated in the early phases of implementation.

• The relatively high confidence of the pastoral leaders in the project and the government. This stems from the fact that the Mauritanian government is predominantly a government of Moor pastoralists. Most government staff are linked to pastoralism, and have the *khaima* ("under the tent") as common reference.

The land area per PO in Mauritania is quite large and the project has not paid adequate attention to local group formation around water points. The project has yet to think of grazing schemes. It does not have the necessary technical personnel in sufficient quantities. Yet the project has set an ambitious target of 101 new POs before it has fully consolidated those already set-up. The expanded program's demands for professional resources cannot possibly be met by the Mauritanian government in the short run. The Mauritanian project will benefit more by going through a pilot phase with the present POs to develop a pool of resource persons at all levels before expanding further. In Mauritania, while the political will and enthusiasm are high, the professional resources for project planning and implementation are still scarce.

Stages in PO Formation

What lessons of timing can be drawn from the four countries regarding PO models and the roles and functions POs could be expected to perform? Should the POs deal with most aspects of pastoral development simultaneously? Should there be a gradual expansion in activities? What different elements should a pastoral institution building program include to support the PO formation?

The main conclusion is that there are no universal models of POs for the West African drylands. The appropriate form will depend on the local circumstances, and the objectives of the development program. Ideally the functions of the different POs should evolve from local needs and priorities through a participatory process. For example, food security and water point management measures could be regarded as appropriate "rallying points" by the pastoralists in the more arid and nomadic areas of Niger, while a revolving fund for veterinary drug stores and training of pastoral agents in animal health would be more highly appreciated by pastoralists in the semi-humid and agro-pastoral conditions of Senegal. A flexible system, involving different levels, forms and functions of POs, may best serve the pastoralists in a given locality.

POs should be encouraged to expand their services and activities in pace with the development of their capacity and economic viability.

Although there is no simple model, there are some common elements and stages in the formation of POs for NRM. The sequence, timing and introduction of new activities will necessarily change from one locality to another-depending on local resources, site-specifity of the development problems, and on external factors. The institution building process may be conceived as a continuum involving five main stages spread over a time span depending on the socio-political environment and other logistical factors.

Stage 1 - identification (1-2 years):

• initial dialogue and mobilization,

• agreements on problem areas and general principles for NRM,

• assessment of local capacity and priorities for NRM,

• election of PO board, delineation of land,

• identification of wells (types, ownership, functions, maintenance needs) and needs for new wells,

• establishment of management committees at village or settlement level particularly for water point management—but in general as building blocks for NRM at the higher level,

• principles for tenurial contracts,

• animation and introduction to principles of resource management,

• health service and literacy training through national programs outside the frame of the PO program,

• support to basic infrastructure and other services (animation, animal health, NRM);

Stage 2 - motivation and mobilization (2-3 years):

• introduction of membership fee systems,

• establishment of PO bank account,

• training and mobilization of board members and traditional leaders in NRM,

• economic planning, accounting, literacy, training of pastoral agents,

• remuneration systems for pastoral agents,

• establishment of low-cost pastoral centers on cost-sharing principles,

• identification of sites for well construction,

• assessment of principles for transferring government wells to PO-managed wells;

Stage 3 - expansion (3-5 years):

• intensive training of management committees and PO board members,

• introduction of revolving fund for veterinary pharmacies to the best-functioning POs, water development,

• transfer of government wells to PO wells,

• introduction of simple grazing management principles, systems of water charges, grazing fees, and fines for illegal actions, more intensive government support;

Stage 4 - consolidation and further expansion (5-10 years):

• training and government services to continue at high intensity, new activities to be introduced depending on performance and needs such as food security, gardening/agro-forestry, marketing, animal fattening, milk production;

Stage 5 - self-management (10-20 years): gradual reduction of government support according to the economic and financial viability and performance of the POs in NRM, but there will always be a role for the government to play in pastoral institution building and NRM.

5. *Women's Role in Pastoral Institution Building and NRM*

Little or no systematic data on gender issues have been gathered in the project areas which reveal the role of pastoral women in the local economies. Field impressions confirm findings from other studies that women's participation in mainstream program activities can be achieved only in the long-term because of cultural and socio-economic constraints.

Present project approaches bypass women almost completely, although women are responsible for important tasks in pastoral production, such as collection of animal fodder and the watering and feeding of small ruminants and young and sick animals. Women process and market milk and milk products and hides, skins and wool. Women participate in agricultural production in the agro-pastoral areas. They fetch water and fuelwood, and are often involved in tree planting and management. They take care of children and carry out strenuous and time-consuming domestic tasks. Their ability to participate in new economic activities and NRM will vary from one local society to another.

In all the pastoral societies visited (Tuareg, Peul, Moor, Wolof, Mandingo), there is a strong division of labor and responsibilities between men and women. Men control most of the animals and are responsible for major decisions related to the herding practices of the household's livestock. Men and older boys usually do the actual herding, especially of cattle and camels. Livestock keeping can, however, be an important source of income for pastoral women. In many societies women own an essential part of the household's herd, obtained either through inheritance or investment of surplus from other economic activities. Among the agro-pastoral Hausa in Maradi (south Niger - outside the project area), women owned 80 percent of total small stock (Raynaut, 1986). The pastoral Kel Dinnik Tuareg women in central Niger owned 20 percent of the domestic animals (Winter, in Swift, 1984). Some of the Tuareg women in ODEM's project area in Mali claimed to own almost 50 percent of the family herd. In other pastoral economies, however, such as the nomadic Wodaabes in Niger and Mali, women have few or no individual rights to livestock. These women do, however, have exclusive milking rights to the family herd and gain important revenues from milk sales.

Few Programs

The projects contain few programs, or none, specifically aimed at improving the living conditions of women and mobilizing them into the POs. As a general rule, the limited number of women's programs evident in the areas were financed outside the projects assisted by the World Bank, usually by bilateral donors or NGOs. These programs are often autonomous projects under a national women's program, but in some cases they report direct to the management of the livestock projects. Many of these women's programs are based on stereotyped ideas of women's economic roles. They are often concerned with human health services and handicrafts, and seldom reflect women's actual responsibilities in livestock keeping, agro-pastoralism and resource management. In many cases they are based on the formation of women's groups, organized with a board consisting of president, vice-president, secretary, accountant and so on. The office bearers are often in the age range of 50 to 60 years and from the well-to-do families. They are normally appointed by men. Training, credit, or other services are channelled through these groups. These women's program activities are seldom functionally integrated into the PO formation process or other project activities.

Some examples of these programs are training of midwives at the PO-level (ODEM, Mali, and Niger), credit for production and marketing of local handicrafts (Mali, Mauritania, and Senegal), credit and extension for gardening (Mauritania, Mali, Senegal), tree-planting (Senegal, Mauritania), and sand dune stabilization (Mauritania).

The women's programs are often small-scale with limited impact on women and local living conditions. For example, at several pilot gardening schemes the women had put considerable labor and time into the construction of wooden fences to protect against animals. Because of lack of water and irrigation, and soil-related factors, the yields were often very low. As isolated development projects, these schemes would have little positive impact on the women's living conditions. At the same time, crop production and crop-livestock integration seem to be areas in which pastoral women can play an important role in the future.

The women do not take part in the village-level meetings organized by project staff and are thus excluded from direct participation in the process of establishing the POs. There are no formal links between the women's groups and state-sponsored POs, although the office-bearers in both institutions often come from the same families. In several cases the president of the women's group was married to the village chief who was president of the local PO. These informal links provide the women with possibilities for indirect influence on decisionmaking in the POs. According to the PO presidents interviewed, there are no formal barriers against a woman joining a PO board. But there was only one female PO board member in all the countries visited.

It is difficult to assess the overall impact on pastoral women of the PO formation and related project activities with no base line data and very little evaluation data available on gender issues. It seems likely that components such as well construction, veterinary services, and rangeland management have little direct effect on women's living conditions. Only in Senegal have as many as 10 percent of the people attending literacy programs been women. A few pastoral women have participated in such exercises in Mali and Niger.

It is also doubtful that women's access to credit has improved. During field work for this study, women often confronted the researchers with demands for credit to start income-generating activities. A common aim was to invest in livestock for their own herds. In several cases in Niger and Mali, initiatives by the women themselves to get credit for livestock or agricultural activities had been turned down by the project management.

It is likely, however, that women benefit indirectly from improved animal health services, establishment of PO veterinary drug stores, and improved water supply although there are no data to confirm this.

The projects may have negative impacts on the women. Among the sedentary Peul in Mali (Boni PO) the workload for women increased after the project started, when women were involved in fetching water and concrete for construction of a dam. Women are also responsible for food preparation for the PO meetings and visitors to the POs. A particular problem arises with the introduction of pastoral cooperatives for commercialization of milk and milk products in Mali, when there are no female members of the cooperative. Sale and marketing of milk products are traditionally women's domain. Will the pastoral women lose this income with the establishment of the cooperatives?

New Roles

Significant changes taking place in social organization and local production systems in the pastoral areas have major implications for the division of labor and responsibilities between men and women.

The increase in labor migration of men, for example, leaves the women and children with a significant increase in work traditionally performed by men. Women must often spend more time on domestic work because of increased competition for and scarcity of water, animal fodder, and fuelwood. In agricultural areas where land pressure has increased, women have often lost their traditional land rights. In some societies, for example Tuareg, pastoral men and women have lost their traditional privileged socio-economic positions. Among recently settled Tuareg in Mali, the formerly wealthy noblewomen have become impoverished, and only a few can now afford to keep Bellah servants to do domestic and agricultural work. Traditionally, the noblewomen were brought up with an aversion to physical labor, spending most of their time socializing or making handicrafts. Now, they have serious problems in adapting to new and often harsh living conditions, particularly since they lack both training and experience in agriculture and do not possess the necessary inputs to start cropping activities.

On the other hand, the increased number of households headed by women provide the women with greater influence over household decisionmaking. In the absence of their men, the women increasingly have to take important herd and resource-management decisions and represent their men in decisionmaking bodies. It is uncertain, however, to what degree the deserted women gain control over their men's herds and direct benefits from sales of animals and animal products. With increased education and exposure to urban societies, cultural values and attitudes among younger pastoralists to the traditional role of women are also changing. The revival of Islamic fundamentalism may, however, counter some of these processes.

Recommendations

The full participation of women in POs can only be achieved in the long-term. It will first require fundamental attitudinal changes at all levels, from the local level to the project level, the national level, and donor level. Recommendations to facilitate this process are

- More research and data-gathering on gender issues should be carried out as part of the pastoral development programs to make the role of women in resource management visible, particularly in relation to the influence of the pastoral women in decisionmaking.
- Gender issues should become an integrated concern of program planning, implementation and evaluation.
- Gender issues should be addressed in project progress reports, supervision and evaluation reports.
- Female staff should be strengthened at all levels in the pastoral programs.
- Training and awareness-raising on gender issues among both male and female staff should be institutionalized in the implementing agencies.
- More women should be encouraged to join training courses in literacy, economic planning and management, accounting, agro-pastoralism, and NRM and to become pastoral development agents to work among women in their own areas.
- The World Bank and other donors should encourage the inclusion of women's programs to stimulate income-generation among women, for example, credit schemes.
- In societies where pastoral women have a relatively high status, the programs should

encourage the participation of women in PO-formation and other mainstream program efforts.

- In societies where women have a relatively low status, the programs should support the formation of women's groups and encourage interaction between these groups and the new POs.

6. The Role of Traditional Institutions

To what extent do traditional cultural institutions operate today? Can traditional customs help to strengthen modern pastoral organizations?

Pastoralists in the Sahel have always been organized in tribes, sub-tribes, clans, lineages, and extended families. Descent as well as affiliation are still organizational principles. The genealogical principle for most nomadic pastoralist groups is patriarchy, which implies agnatic kinship groups with obligations and rights for members of a group and subgroups. Most pastoralists in the Sahel are patrilineal, for instance the Arab, the Moor, and the Peul. Cattle, sheep, goats, camels, other animals, and material goods, are inherited from father to son and from father to daughter and sometimes to other kin members and even non-members. A few groups like the Tuareg of Central Sahara in Mali and Niger are matrilineal.

There is a collective solidarity within cohesive groups of pastoralists which is important in resource management decisions. In Mauritania the collective solidarity is called *asabiya* in the Arab dialect, Hassaniya (Bonte 1985). The Moors constitute social groups with this principle. Social proximity and social distance are expressed through *asabiya*, which is present also in state-sponsored POs. The Moor tribe is organized around the distinction between the center, the *nasab* of the dominant group, and periphery (Bonte 1985). In many Peul societies the tribe and sub-tribe is called *lenyol*, and the sub-group of the *lenyol* is called *tarde*.

It is normally easier to organize people who are already members of the same sub-group of a tribe than to organize people who are genealogically distant. It can be a real problem to unite people from different tribes, or from different ethnic groups altogether, into one and the same PO. But in some places it has been done, building on ties of neighborhood and friendship, or political alliances between pastoral and agro-pastoral groups. In Mauritania, Bonte (1991) observed Moors and Peuls co-existing in the same POs, both groups being represented in the PO leadership. This situation improves local communication and conflict resolution.

Cultural Factors in PO Formation

For the Peul (FulBe, Pulaar, Farfarou, Jafun, Wodaabe) the key concept is *pulaaku*, the pastoral code for proper behavior, which applies for most Peul groups from Senegal in the west to Sudan in the east. It is a social as well as an individual moral code. To follow *pulaaku* is to follow "the Fulani way". There is social cohesion involved in this cultural concept. It implies social rules, and a harmonizing of human relations. In the Peul language, Fulfulde, some important human characteristics and concepts are:

- *Hakkiilo* - "good use of the world", including natural resources, intelligence in finding grass, water, and leading the group properly.
- *Semtudum* - not to hurt others, self-control, not to eat too much.

- *Bernde* - "heart", to be brave, have courage in life.
- *Munyal* - patience and endurance.
- *Pasali* - the right "measure", to be satisfied with little, and to stay in one's proper place or within limits.

These principles guide people's decisions and actions, and ensure survival as pastoralists. The *pulaaku*, for example, dictates what to do in times of droughts, diseases, and death, as well as in good years. Richer pastoralists are obliged to lend or give away animals to poorer pastoralists in need. This redistributive system is also embedded in Islam, in the *shari'a* law system which is widespread in pastoral zones of the Sahel. A Peul virtue like *munyal* (patience) may be conservative and status-quo like, whereas another virtue *bernde* (courage, to be brave) may be mobilized as a virtue to inspire new ways of thinking and acting. The active promotion of these virtues is as yet untried in pastoral institution building.

Traditional and New Leadership

The local Peul institutions of chief and sub-chief are still important and are certain to reappear in the POs studied. The *Jooro* in Mali is the Peul chief who controls access to the Delta pastures. In Niger we find the *laamido* (big chief) and the *ardo* (small chief, literally: "The one who walks ahead"). The traditional leaders still have major influence on collective and individual decisionmaking. They are always consulted when important decisions are to be taken. The PO leaders are often kinsmen, or related people, frequently from the nobility. These social and political institutions can be used for promoting state-sponsored POs.

Traditional leaders can, however, also be a constraint to new POs. Conflicts have been reported between traditional elderly leaders and more literate younger men. There may be generational conflicts and competition for power and leadership posts in the POs. Literacy is often a decisive factor. In several cases, elderly traditional leaders had been replaced by younger more dynamic and literate men. The one female PO board member was a Tuareg woman in northern Mali, who reflects the matrilinity of the Tuareg society, and the relatively high status of women.

In Niger, it was seen how the pastoralists' distrust of government is rooted in historical experience. It is a paradox that the nomadic pastoral societies with the least established communication with the state, are those with the highest need for new institutions. At the same time skepticism toward the government is high among these groups, for instance the Wodaabe of Niger (Bovin and Manger (ed) 1990). There is a need for POs through which pastoralists, especially the more "stateless", independent and egalitarian tribal pastoralists, true nomads, can communicate with governments. Agro-pastoral and settled agricultural populations have more established contacts with the government. They are often more literate, communicate more easily, and find their interests more readily accepted.

Territorial Organizations

According to Swift (1988) there are two broad patterns of the territorial organization of pastoral societies in West Africa. First are the territorial systems based on lineage or class organization, in which membership in a social group confers the right to use pasture in the territory of that group. Often the dominant group would exclude other pastoral groups from using its water and grazing resources. This system is found among the hierarchical societies of the Moors and Tuaregs, and some agro-pastoral Peul. Although weakened over recent decades, these institutions still determine main patterns of spatial distribution of pastoral groups, their ownership of water rights, and their willingness to accept new forms of territorial organization.

In contrast, some pastoral societies in dryland West Africa have no traditional territorial organization, and no specific claim to rangeland areas other than occupation on a first-come, first-served basis (Swift 1988). Sometimes this may be combined with ownership of wells by the individuals who constructed them. The nomadic pastoral Peul of Northern Niger, and in particular the Wodaabe, follow the latter system. Social organization among the Wodaabe is very flexible. Wodaabe groups have traditions for using public wells or making a Hausa dig a deep well which becomes the common property of the group. The water right is then confined strictly to this group (Swift 1988).

Traditional Systems of Redistribution

The Wodaabe of Niger have a system called *habbanaayi* or *nanganaayi* (Bovin 1990: 48), "the third cow", which is a borrowed milking cow that is placed in the borrower's herd temporarily. When the cow has given birth to two calves, the owner will claim the cow back. The borrower, often a patrilineal kinsman, will keep the two or three calves as a gift. Another system of redistribution of animals is the *diilaayi* or "milking a cow for a season"; a time-limited loan. After years of severe drought these systems have proved efficient. They have saved many poor pastoralists, and reintegrated them into the pastoral social group. This system normally works within a tribal sub-group, not across tribal groups. The animals normally circulate within the primary lineage group. These systems also have limited efficiency in times of serious drought or famine. POs which cut across ethnic lines can play a role to this end.

The Moors of Mauritania have a system in which rich animal owners are obliged to give animals to poor, a system embedded in the Muslim code.

There are also traditions for mobilizing work parties or age-groups according to the age grades of young women with a female leader or young men with a male leader. Such institutions could be used within POs. It is interesting to note that the new names given to POs in the local languages were often taken from these traditional groups, the name meaning "the group of age mates".

Traditional grassroots institutions, like the reciprocity and redistributive systems *habbanaayi* and *diilaayi* among the Peul, are still viable. Planners of pastoral institution building programs should learn from these systems, and use them in the promotion of POs and NRM activities.

7. *Recommendations*

Pastoral institution building for improved resource management in the Sahel is a long-term cumulative and participatory process. It is a means of empowering pastoralists, developing livestock, and promoting sustainable NRM. From these premises a shift is recommended from the present finite project approach to a program approach guided by a long-term perspective with a genuine commitment from the governments. The major aim of these programs should be to promote improved NRM and pastoral development at the local level by enabling POs to strengthen their authority and control over the management of water, rangeland and other local resources.

The governments and donors should reconceptualize pastoral institution building with reference to the conditions of an enabling environment for POs and site-specificities such as type of pastoralism, resource conflicts, and socio-economic features. The approach adopted should seek to promote wider participation of local groups in POs by letting solutions to local problems emerge from below. PO components of individual projects should be linked to the long-term program in ways that ensure their continuity beyond the project periods. The overall approach should include drought contingency plans to minimize herd losses and their consequences including displacement of pastoralists.

Approach and Planning

A more explicit focus on PO formation and NRM in project preparation and appraisal is needed to make these aspects of pastoral development better understood and appreciated at government and project implementation levels. Included should be a brief description of the rationale behind the PO formation, an outline of the approaches for establishing the POs, and a clear differentiation between service activities (animal health, marketing, provisioning, drought contingency measures) and NRM activities, and their respective logistical requirements.

NRM activities should be further differentiated with reference to water management, regulation of grazing, and long-term conservation practices including management of trees. There should be a clear identification of available and appropriate NRM methods and techniques and the logistical needs, including training, for their successful adoption. Such a detailed differentiation of management functions is a prerequisite for evolving appropriate organization models and defining the stages of evolution of POs. The NRM activities adopted by a PO would depend on the local conditions and the competence available within the group. For instance, water points provide a basis for small cohesive groups and their management can become the first main activity. Range patrolling may also begin at this stage. However, range management and conservation may be adopted at the next or a later stage when the group has gained adequate management skills and motivation through animation and training.

Budget allocations for the PO component should be increased so that activities like mobilization, literacy, training and leadership development receive the high priority they deserve. Allocations for these programs should be omitted from rate of return calculations. Ideally they should be exempt from it, but remain subject to systematic monitoring and evaluation of progress in organization and local competence-building.

Pre-program requirements

A successful formulation of the PO components of a program presupposes a good information base about the communities concerned and their production systems. In this regard, the following basic requirements are needed:

- A deeper knowledge of the socio-economic and cultural conditions of the target groups and their production systems in terms of the type of pastoralism, mobility patterns and interdependencies, availability and types of water points, and rangeland conditions, including gender roles and the internal structural changes caused by dispossession and the rise of absentee herd ownership. It is essential to assess the changes taking place at local levels in resource-use patterns caused by voluntary settlement and the trend toward agro-pastoralism.
- A better grasp of the pastoralists' perceptions and priorities of their institutional needs and the links between those perceptions and priorities and NRM.
- An assessment of the existing forms of traditional cohesive groups and their potentials as starting points for POs.
- An assessment of the status of women in these groups. Two important questions are: are they recognized by men as resource managers and do they participate in decisionmaking?
- An assessment of the model and approach for PO formation, including the selection of main functions ('rallying points') and criteria for PO membership.
- An assessment of the literacy levels of the traditional leaders and potential leaders with reference to the minimum literacy required to play leadership roles in state-sponsored POs.
- An assessment of the institutional and human resources competence and capacity of the implementing agencies, and preparation of systematic programs to strengthen the efficiency of these institutions to meet the objectives of PO development and NRM.
- An assessment of the policy and regulatory framework for pastoral institution building, including an assessment of the capacity of the government's administrative, educational, and health services in the project area.

Given these requirements, a stronger involvement of personnel with competence in rural sociology, development anthropology, institutional economics, NRM and law is recommended in the pre-project, project planning and early implementation phases.

Government Commitment

Each country should develop a national program based on decentralized regional programs and well-established priorities. Project interventions to assist pastoral institution building should be integrated into the regional and national programs to secure the government's commitment and to ensure the continuity of the institution building process. The government should take the following steps to facilitate an enabling environment for POs.

Tenurial reforms

The formalization of clearly defined and legally defensible communal rights to rangeland, pasture and trees, and water should be treated as an urgent priority in all countries. Tenurial reform should pay special attention to protection of dry season pastures from intrusion by agriculturalists. It should include clear definitions of obligations of the resource users and guidelines to resolve intra and inter-community and inter-sectoral resource-use conflicts. Spatial demarcation of rangeland for particular POs should be flexible enough to permit reciprocity between POs and transhumance. All existing public water points constructed by the government should be converted into communal waterpoints of the POs.

Government's failure to provide and enforce appropriate tenurial rights will strengthen insecurity among pastoralists, and reduce their motivation to adopt NRM practices and share costs of construction of water points and infrastructure. The main problem may not be to define formal rights, which may be based on customary usufruct rights, long-term communal lease, or transferable private rights, but to find effective means of enforcement. The government should be prepared to assist POs with enforcement of tenurial rights until such time as they are able to handle the matter on their own. Governments' enforcement efforts should be accompanied by a campaign to inform the people concerned, both pastoralists and agriculturalists, about the tenurial systems, and help them learn about their rights and obligations.

National coordination unit

A coordinating unit should be established at the national level, for example in the Ministry of Rural Development, to coordinate pastoral institution building and NRM efforts in the pastoral areas. It could be co-located with, for example, a unit for coordinating NRM matters, as proposed by Lewis (1989). The role of the unit would be to collect and analyze results and experiences from pilot operations, mainly within the country, but also from other countries, identify, and assess site-specific lessons for possible replication or generalization. It should also identify and assess key political and institutional issues. The unit should preferably have multi-disciplinary competence, and be provided funds for recruitment of local or foreign experts.

Decentralization of tenurial reform

Implementation of tenurial reform should be decentralized to the regional level with sufficient authority to grant communal rights to land and to adjudicate conflicts within pastoral communities and between agriculture, pastoralism and wildlife. The implementation process should involve POs from the beginning. The decentralization should be carried out with due regard to coordination of the roles of the local governmental and the administrative authorities. The central government and donors should be more willing to delegate authority to lower levels and encourage decentralization of all program functions and responsibilities.

The final responsibility for a regional program should lie with one institution which should be delegated sufficient authority to be in constant dialogue with pastoralists, convene meetings of regional and local bodies, prepare budgets and manage the funds received from POs and from the National Fund. Project level components in PO formation and development should be directly linked to the regional programs which in turn are linked to the national program.

Pastoral development centers

Pastoral development centers should be set-up at sub-project levels, similar to Niger's CP but with more professional resources and facilities to undertake continuous training of pastoralists. The centers should provide assistance in resource planning and in resolving local resource conflicts. An adequate number of competent and committed *animateurs* (Pastoral Community Development Agents) should be posted at this level to inform and mobilize pastoralists and train pastoral agents. These Centers should facilitate communication between POs and help make implementing agencies become more accountable to the POs. Ways must be found to reduce transport costs of animation and extension, possibly by use of camels and horses.

Pastoral community development agents (PCDAs)

The programs should strengthen efforts to train male and female PCDAs, chosen from among pastoralists to work in their own areas. They should be given an integrated training in rural mobilization, including mobilization of women, animal health and NRM, and in training pastoral leaders in NRM, economic planning and elementary book-keeping. The training of both new and traditional pastoral leaders, should be given high priority. The costs of training PCDAs and their remuneration for an initial period should be borne by the regional programs. After the initial period, which may vary according to circumstances, the POs and the individual pastoralists receiving the services of a PCDA should remunerate the agent according to standard rates fixed regionally.

Participation

The projects should encourage popular participation in planning and implementation, particularly in those NRM activities which have lower priority among pastoralists, such as tree-planting, fire or wind-break establishment, and soil conservation.

Governments should, with donor assistance, develop more systematic approaches to the strengthening of institutional capacities in program and policy formulation, implementation and monitoring. Strengthening of competence in rural sociology and environmental management at the local and national levels is particularly required. Competence in environmental management requires upgrading of technical skills, acquisition of environmental tools such as maps, environmental data, simple monitoring systems, environmental guidelines and check-lists as well as strengthening of managerial capacities. Government institutions should strengthen efforts to coordinate policies and programs. Coordination is also crucial with the national programs for functional literacy, education, health, and rural infrastructure.

Orientation for professional staff

Government personnel performing various tasks in the pastoral sector should be given obligatory orientation courses on the social, economic, ecological, and technical aspects of pastoralism in the Sahel. Such courses should address the need for attitudinal changes among government officials at all levels toward pastoralists, the role of women in pastoral and rural development and the centrality of the producers in institution building.

Foreign experts

Governments should carefully identify their needs for professional resources in pastoral institution building and NRM according to the regional programs and assess the local availability. They should seek foreign assistance to meet the shortfalls via visiting experts and develop local professional resources. Foreign experts should be required to play a more active role in the personnel development programs of the institutions to which they are attached.

Marketing

The projects have in a few cases attempted to help PO members in the marketing of livestock and livestock products, without much success, partly because local traders were operating more efficiently. The pastoral development programs could, however, help POs to organize group sales of animals, to obtain market information, and bargain for better prices from the local traders.

Monitoring and evaluation

The monitoring of the progress in PO formation and NRM should be strengthened both at the level of the National Coordinating Unit and at project level. This is particularly necessary for all pilot operations. These operations should, from time to time, undergo a more thorough evaluation. A simple and cost-effective but sufficiently comprehensive set of indicators should be developed to assess progress. These indicators should include membership charges, activities undertaken, revenue generation and financial performance, progress in literacy and training, resource conflicts and resolution, and changes in herd size and composition. PO leaders should be trained to collect, process, and transmit this information to the level above.

The main elements of an enabling environment should be in place before the start-up of a pastoral development program. The projects do not have leverage for creating substantial changes in policy and institutional frameworks in the course of a short implementation period. Loan covenants are no substitute for appropriate policies. Government commitment should be translated into action as recommended.

Restrictions on absentee herd ownership

Large-scale absentee herd ownership should be discouraged as it is not conducive to livestock development, NRM, and pastoral institution building. With the attribution of tenure rights, POs should be authorized to charge higher fees for water, pasture, and other facilities extended to herds belonging to absentee owners and non-members. The national program should also include contingency funds for herd reconstitution credit to encourage owner-herders.

Literacy

National literacy programs for adults of both sexes and primary education for children should be extended to pastoral areas. Such programs should be adapted to the prevailing daily and seasonal patterns of pastoral life. The experiences of the literacy programs of the projects may be helpful in innovating workable literacy programs. The administration of these programs should be in the hands of regional and sub-regional authorities.

Public health

Basic public health facilities should be considerably strengthened and extended to pastoral areas through national programs outside the frame of the pastoral development programs. Access to basic social services and basic education is crucial both for fostering economic development and addressing poverty.

Rural infrastructure

Adequate public investment should be directed to pastoral areas to improve communication and facilitate transport and flow of marketing, environmental, and other information. Rural infrastructure development should be carried out through decentralized public investment budgets, at low cost and with the participation of the beneficiary communities.

Participation of women

Governments and international agencies should recognize the importance of pastoral and agro-pastoral women as economic actors and resource managers, and explicitly integrate their role in pastoral development programs. Depending on the social context and the local status of women, activities should be directed to the strengthening of women's groups and programs and to encouraging the participation of women in the POs and mainstream program activities. Efforts should be made to increase the female staff at all levels. All personnel, irrespective of sex, should be made more aware of gender issues as an aspect of rural development. The monitoring and evaluation system should cover the gender dimension.

Privatization

A gradual privatization of veterinary health services and drug handling and selling should be encouraged. The POs should participate as corporate bodies in the privatization of animal health services and food supply. Credit schemes to establish revolving funds may require changes in credit policies and in the attitudes of the national banks toward POs.

A national fund

The government should establish a fund for its National Pastoral Institution Building Program from public and private domestic and donor sources. The replenishment of the fund could come from import duties on animal drugs and inputs, or other taxes. The fund should be distributed to the regional programs according to a set of agreed priorities.

Revenue-generation and cost-sharing

POs should be made partners in the construction of community-level infrastructure, for example, water points, pastoral development centers, PO offices, clinics, stores and local roads, by supplying labor and sharing the financial costs. POs should be authorized to collect animal taxes from members, and fines from persons caught for unauthorized cutting of trees, as means to raise funds at the local level. POs should be given better guidance in increasing their revenue-generation through membership fees, water charges, grazing fees, and management of services like distribution of animal drugs and essential goods. There should be a three-level, differentiated scale of fees that favors herds owned by members over non-members. Absentee herd owners should pay extra as a partial compensation for their non-participation in POs and their activities. All POs should contribute to the Regional Pastoral Institution Building Program. POs should be encouraged to strengthen their organization at national levels. The national level organizations should be encouraged to take an active role in livestock development and generation of funds through, for example, importation, distribution, and sales of veterinary drugs and animal inputs.

Donor Assistance

International donors like the World Bank should pay greater attention to compliance with policy and institutional preconditions for PO development by the governments. They should, through policy dialogue and direct support, encourage the governments to strengthen the policy level, and supervise implementation of tenurial reforms and decentralization. They should ensure an adequate level of delegation of authority to the regional and local levels. The World Bank should strengthen its management procedures and field supervision of the PO formation process and NRM activities.

Donors should channel support to pastoral institution building through the national program but to specific locations so that progress can be monitored more concretely. Linkages with the regional and national programs should be established as a precondition. Donors supporting pastoral institution building in a particular country should with the agreement and guidance of the government coordinate their efforts to avoid duplication, and maximize impact. Coordination should extend to evaluation of missions and field research, and to documentation and transmission of information.

8. *Further Research and Follow-Up*

There are great uncertainties about how to address resource management in the pastoral zone (Steeds 1989). This comparative review may provide some new insights. But the pilot work in PO formation under these projects has in most cases not been completed. New evaluation studies will be required when these experiences are more advanced, and the findings should be fed back to the governments and donors in a systematic way.

The World Bank is the leading development institution assisting governments in the pastoral zones of West Africa. Other donors have virtually abandoned these areas (Steeds 1989). Given the overall reduction in bilateral donor support and the increased competition for donor funding, bilateral donor support to the Sahelian drylands is not likely to increase in the foreseeable future.

Involvement in pastoral development and NRM is a long-term commitment. The short-term presence of many donors has been a main constraint to development in the drylands (Nekby 1990). If the World Bank pulls out or continues to lower investments, other donors are likely to disappear completely. This would also imply lower government support to these areas. Overall, there could be domino effects with severe social, economic and environmental consequences. Recent events in Mali, Niger and Mauritania prove that political stabilization depends on the full participation of pastoral and agro-pastoral communities in political and economic affairs. Such participation requires continued external investments and government support to the pastoral areas.

The World Bank's comparative advantage in the pastoral zones is in the areas of policy dialogue and institutional-development at national level: improving the policy environment with respect to price and marketing policies and incentives, investment priorities, land tenure and natural resources management policies, institutional and infrastructural development.

As a major supplier of financial resources for livestock and pastoral development, providing advice on policy as well as technical matters, the World Bank exerts considerable influence on government thinking. This is particularly the case when new or complicated policy and program elements are introduced, which lack clearly articulated strategies for development in the pastoral zones. The World Bank should be given credit for setting pastoral institution building and NRM on the political agenda in these countries.

However, the World Bank has no comparative advantage in the areas of local level expertise required for pastoral institution building and NRM. The Bank has developed some, but still insufficient internal competence to deal with these matters in which it is still dependant upon external sociological and environmental sources. If the Bank continues to support investment in pastoral areas, it should develop its internal competence in these subjects or look for partnerships with other bilateral donors and NGOs better equipped to handle grass-roots operations. One could foresee a model in which the governments (with World Bank support) develop an appropriate national policy and institutional framework for pastoral institution building and initiate pilot operations for PO formation at the local level. Drawing upon lessons from the pilot phase, bilateral donors and NGOs could be encouraged to support the extension of the programs to other areas. This model is faced with two problems:

(a) there are very few organizations with extensive experience in pastoral institution building and NRM, and (b) it raises new issues of collaboration and coordination between donors as well as between donors and government agencies.

To improve support to policy reforms, the World Bank should consider strengthening its management and procedures in the following areas:

• To ensure continuity of in-country support for pastoral development programs, the Bank should, as far as possible, obtain guarantees from government of long-term commitment, prior to start-up.

• A detailed project approach should be changed to a more flexible "program approach", including drought contingency plans for emergency assistance to the pastoralists to limit famine and dispossession of animals. A more flexible design would require more intensive supervision.

• Strengthening of internal competence in sociology and anthropology on pastoral development issues would improve design and implementation, and limit unintended diversion of benefits.

The Bank should also consider:

• Improvement of its own competence to handle the technical and managerial aspects of NRM.

• Improvement of coordination of Bank efforts with those of other donors. Nekby (1990) has observed that in the absence of a clearly articulated government strategy projects tend to reflect a series of diverse donor perceptions with resulting efforts that are often confused and contradictory, ineffective and discontinuous.

Many Questions Still Unanswered

In many areas, the original projects must be considered as pilots, raising as many questions as they have answered.

A second phase of this study should involve longer field work, more substantial data gathering, and draw extensively on local researchers and project staff. Ideally it should be preceded by the establishment of a monitoring and evaluation system at the program level to overcome the present basic information constraints.

The following topics particularly require further research and study.

• How can traditional institutions for social cohesion and economic cooperation be used in the promotion of POs? How do traditional territorial organizations operate today and how could they form the basis for state-sponsored POs? This study has provided a brief introduction to this topic.

• What is the future economic viability of pastoralism? Can economic viability of the POs be sufficient to sustain NRM and development service functions? What income-generating activities, other than membership fees, should POs be encouraged to start? How should a pastoral development program assist the POs to improve financial viability? Has the establishment of a wildlife or tourism component been considered as an income-generating NRM activity?

• More explicit data on pastoralists' present and potential economic contribution to their national economies would appeal more to national economic self-interest. An appeal on these grounds might be more useful in securing necessary legislation or continuity of funding from governments than an image of pastoralists as a destitute environmental threat.

• To what extent is population growth a key factor in the decline of pastoralism? Is absentee ownership an indication that pastoralism is in terminal decline? A calculation of food production from livestock in arid rangeland shows that 100 ha devoted solely to pastoralism can provide enough food (calories as milk and meat) for about two or three people but one cultivated ha can provide a similar amount of food (calories). In this instance the cultivation of one percent of the pastoralist area increases the human carrying capacity by about 100 percent. It is important to bear in mind that cultivation is a rational response to the problem of population growth, where the livestock-carrying capacity of the given area has reached or exceeded the limit. The dramatically greater efficiency of crop farming (agropastoralism) compared to pure pastoralism as a system of food production is the basis of this response.

Perhaps then, emphasis should be placed on the problems and issues of agro-pastoralists and small crop farmers, because even if pastoralists are given exclusive use of a defined area of grazing they will have to face these decisions in time unless they control population growth. In many areas of the Sahel, the growth of population is pushing toward the biological limits. An important part of the social and economic planning of these areas must include a recognition that there are such limits, and of where they lie. A future study should address this issue.

• Could livestock marketing be improved to become a significant factor in the viability of POs and pastoralism?

• On what criteria should land-use planning and decisions to convert grazing land to crop land be made? Based on econometric modelling, a study in the Niger delta of Mali concludes that pastoral production is economically superior to rice cultivation on the bourgou grassland (CABO 1990). What factors affect the conversion of grazing land to crop land in such cases?

• How serious are the rangeland degradation and resource-use conflicts in the pastoral areas? There is a need to find ways to measure rangeland degradation more precisely than through the much used concepts of rangeland "carrying capacity" which is conceptually ambiguous and difficult to apply in practice. Different commentators have pointed to the need for a more rigorously defined concept of rangeland degradation based on measurement of soil loss. They have pointed to the importance of episodic events, especially rainfall variability, in causing both vegetation change and fluctuations in livestock numbers in the drylands.

• To what extent will the introduction of tenure rights really encourage long-term investments in range management and NRM? The experiences from Senegal are mixed, but do indicate that improved rangeland management and conflict resolution took place. Private ownership may not be a guarantee of better rangeland management, according to some authors (Toulmin 1991, Swift 1988 and 1989, Shanmugaratnam and others 1989).

• How can POs be provided legally defensible tenure rights as a sound basis for more long-term investment in range management and NRM, while maintaining sufficient flexibility to allow for traditional reciprocal grazing arrangements with neighboring groups receiving lower rainfall during certain periods?

• How can systems of water charges and revenue-generation by wells committees be strengthened so that wells can be amortized and payment for maintenance secured? At present, for example, the cost of a new well (about 2 million FCFA in Mali) cannot be raised by a local society. A cost-sharing agreement with government is therefore necessary.

• What technologies are readily adoptable for improving rangeland productivity, and the resilience of pastoral and agro-pastoral systems?

• What are the labor requirements throughout the season for various NRM activities, what should be undertaken by POs, and what should be the responsibility of individual households? Is there a danger of overloading the POs with new activities? What role should the central and local governments play in future NRM activities?

• What are the potential benefits in the short and long-term at the household level, and how do benefits from NRM activities compare with benefits from alternative use of local labor and resources?

• Are pastoralists and pastoral areas within the PO projects better off than those in ajacent areas outside the projects? Other communities should be visited and comparisons made. What support is being offered by other groups such as NGOs in fields such as literacy and animal health care that might continue to assist if governments fail to do so?

• How should the POs relate to the local

government? A trend toward decentralization and devolution of authority to rural councils elected by the local population may create tensions between these institutions and POs. Should both the POs and rural councils collect grazing fees or cattle tax? How should the central government divide support between the POs and councils? How should these institutions relate to each other in local decisionmaking regarding development?

Members of a pastoral association in Mauritania

Annex. Land and Water Rights

At the time when this study was conducted, the position of land and water rights as they affect pastoralists in the four countries was summarized as follows:

Mali

Mali has yet to develop comprehensive legal procedure to regularize land and water rights for pastoralists. The institutional challenge is made more formidable by the special importance of the Niger delta for pastoralism, agriculture and fishery. The Malian Land Code of 1986/91 authorizes the regional Commandant to alienate up to a maximum of 10 hectares of state land to a local person for agricultural use. Only the government can grant titles to areas larger than 10 hectares. Obviously the Land Code in its present form is not helpful in solving the problem of pastoral land rights which involve thousands of hectares per PO.

The Niger delta, which is so vital to Malian pastoralists because of its dry season grazing grounds, is an area of multiple land uses, with a variety of formal and informal land tenurial systems and resource conflicts. Lands are privately owned or controlled, communally held and managed, and state-owned in the delta. The state land is *de facto* an open access resource. The major part of the bourgou grasslands, the best pastures in the delta, are privately controlled by Jooros, the traditional Peul (Fulbe) chiefs. There are the traditional village commons called Harima consisting of bourgou grass, privately cultivated rice fields under the aegis of Operation Rice Mopti (ORM), and open access rice lands cultivated by individuals on a temporary basis. Then there are the open access grazing lands. Agriculture has expanded at the expense of grazing lands. More than 50 percent of the original grazing land is cultivated, according to an official of ODEM who has lived in the delta since 1964. In some parts of the delta, ORM's rice polders block the traditional cattle paths. There are intersectoral conflicts, as a result. The Jooros charge the herders large fees for the bourgou grass.

The carrying capacity of the delta has been dramatically exceeded without any signs of regulation of the herd populations moving into it. Since the delta supplies the pastures for the most of the animal populations in the project area for several months of the year, its carrying capacity should be treated as a vital determinant of the sustainable animal population for the whole project area.

Any Malian land tenurial reform for sustainable pastoralism and agriculture in the project area should be cognizant of the delta as an integral part of the larger resource base for pastoral, agro-pastoral, agricultural and fish production. The delineation and legalization of grazing units in the highland have to be part of a larger exercise in institutional reform involving tenurial systems for the sustainable utilization of the resources in the delta by pastoralists, agriculturalists and fishermen. A higher degree of stabilization of pastoralism in the highlands and the regulation of cattle movement into the delta, with a view to minimizing overcrowding in the dry season can contribute to a more sustainable use of the delta's resources. According to some commentators a legalized tenure right could be conferred on the POs by use of the existing law (*le domaine privé de l'Etat/article 5 du Code Forestier*) (IRAM1991).

Mauritania

In Mauritania, a new law on land ownership was enacted on June 5, 1983 and followed by implementation regulations on January 19, 1984. The principal feature of these texts is to abolish all traditional forms of land ownership based on tribal, ethnic, or social factors in favor of property rights prescribed by shari'a, the Islamic law. Under the new law all vacant and undeveloped lands belong to the state. The possibility of the government leasing land to pastoral cooperatives is explicitly recognized. Such land leases can specify all necessary conditions for proper management and development of the lands and all third-party rights, for example access for other pastoral groups in times of drought. Access to "protected" or "classified" lands is regulated under the Forestry Code of December 15, 1982. The Law on Cooperatives of July 18, 1967 provides an appropriate basis for the legal recognition of POs. However, the specifics of the POs and the manner and conditions in which lands would be put at their disposal would have to be determined in each case on the basis of detailed investigations of local conditions. It was concluded at the appraisal stage of the project that the existing legislation provided a workable legal framework for the execution of the project. Although the government has issued a letter (14 August, 1990) giving general recognition of the PO's right to water and grazing resources, supplementary and specific regulations to facilitate its implementation at the PO level have yet to be developed.

Niger

Land legislation in Niger has largely been designed to protect the interests of agriculturalists, often to the disadvantage of herders. Land conversion for farming has gained momentum as former slaves and destitute pastoralists adopt permanent cropping and agro-pastoralism, a trend also found in some parts of the other countries. Law 61-5 (1961) which set a northern limit to farming has not been satisfactorily enforced, and as a result herders are often required to compensate farmers for crop damage caused by their herds even beyond the legally set northern limit for farming. Even though the law permits only herders to cultivate north of the line, traditional farmers do intrude. It has become almost impossible to prevent this as the law does not define "herders" and therefore anybody can qualify (Swift 1984).

As regards water and land rights in the pastoral zone, legislative reforms have yet to be introduced although the *Code Rurale* has been specially set up to draft tenurial reforms. The project area has hundreds of traditional wells which are privately owned with clearly defined and secure rights. The owners observe the established customs of water distribution. The project has converted eighteen open access public wells into "GMP wells". This is a step in the right direction as it has changed open access public wells into locally managed communal wells and has helped to regulate access to the surrounding rangelands. However, in law the GMP wells are still public wells. As a pastoralist put it, "the traditional wells have an insecure physical structure but the owners have secure rights. The opposite is true for the GMP wells—they have secure physical structure but insecure legal rights!".

Conversion of all public wells into GMP wells is an essential first step toward rational range management in Niger. Another consideration is the relative importnce of GMP wells and traditional ones. The creation of public waterpoints by governments in the Sahel made untapped rangelands available to herders but as open access resources. These waterpoints should become common possessions of particular groups if viable communal systems of sustainable pasture and tree management are to become operational. In this regard, Niger's example of GMP wells is of interest to the other countries.

Water and land tenurial reforms in Niger should take privately owned traditional wells and the GMP ones into account as well as the interdependencies between the pastoral and the agro-pastoral zones for grazing and water resources. The 1961 law should be replaced or modified to resolve agriculture-pastoralism conflicts in ways that do not jeopardize the resource security of pastoralists. The *Code Rurale* has proposed that the modern property law is not an appropriate instrument to solve the land and water rights problems of pastoralism in Niger. Emphasizing the communal character of pastoral land and water use and the traditionally prevailing notions of priority rights and reciprocity among pastoralists, it has called for a dialogue between the state and pastoral and agro-pastoral communities to develop the institutional arrangements for sustainable resource use. *Code Rurale* has proposed that public water points should be transferred to the GMPs which would manage them as commons.

Senegal

Most of the pastoral land in Senegal is state property. The law stipulates some strict conditions for alienation of state land to individuals or institutions. Usufruct or private ownership may be granted to a land-user only if the land has been used continuously for several years and "developed" by the user as required by the shari'a. The law does not recognize pastoral use as an activity that "develops" the land. This legal bottle-neck is compounded by the ceiling on the amount of land that may be granted to a person or institution imposed by the National Property Law. The ceiling is too low to permit a legally valid allocation of adequate grazing land to a PO. The legislation is currently under review for reform as the government is anxious to strengthen the legal status of GIEs and POs. Regarding water rights, the open access bore holes constructed by the government in the 1950s and 1960s need to be legally converted into common properties of POs.

The Senegalese Government has introduced a Protocol Agreement between the GIEs and the local government and the project to regulate transhumance of herds of all species in the project area. This Agreement is a formalization of obligations on the part of GIEs to negotiate with the government and obtain approval of access to range and water in areas under PDESO.

Herding for an absentee owner

Bibliography

Abel, N. O. J., and P. M. Blaikie. 1990. "Land Degradation, Stocking Rates and Conservation Policies in the Communal Rangelands of Botswana and Zimbabwe". Pastoral Development Network Paper 29a, ISSN 0951 1911. London: ODI.

Barrier, C. 1988. *Evaluation Rétrospective du Projet de Développement de l'Elevage au Sénégal Oriental (PDESO)*. Paris: CCCE.

Behnke, R. H. 1992. "New Directions in African Range Management Policy." Pastoral Development Network Paper 32c. ODI, London.

Behnke, R. H., and I. Scoones, 1991. *Rethinking Range Ecology: Implications for Rangeland Management in Africa, Overview of Paper Presentations and Discussions at the Technical Meeting on Savanna Development and Pasture Production*, Woburn, London: ODI/IIED.

Bie, S. W. 1990. *Dryland Degradation Measurement Techniques, Environment Department*. World Bank, Washington, D.C.

Bishop, J. 1988. *Indigenous Social Structures, Formal Institutions, and the Management of Renewable Natural Resources in Mali*. The World Bank, Africa Region, Sahelian Department, Agriculture Division, Washington, D.C.

Blakie, P. 1989. *Why and How do Land Users make Land Management Decisions? How can Policies encourage Land Users to make Them Effectively?* Dryland Seminar Paper, World Bank, Washington, D.C.

Bocoum, M. and T. Sanogo. 1988. *Séminaire National Sur les Associations Pastorales et le Développement*. Sujet: "La Gestion de l'Espace Pastoral. Aspects de Politique Foncière." Bamako, Mali.

Bonfiglioli, A. M. 1985. "Evolution de la Propriété Animale chez les Woodaabe du Niger". *Journal des Africanistes* 55: 29-37.

Bonfiglioli, A. M. 1986. *The Pastoral Areas. Problems of Management and Possible Solutions*. Working Paper. Workshop on Desertification Control and Renewable Resources Management in the Sahelian and Sudanian Zones, June 8-14, 1986, Oslo, Norway.

Bonte, P. 1975. "L'Organisation Economique des Touaregs Kel Gress." In R. Cresswell, ed., *Eléments d'Ethnologie*. Paris: Colin.

Bonte, P. 1985. "Ramages Maures." In *Journal des Africanistes*, Musée de l'Homme, Tome 55, Fasc. 1-2, pp 39-52, Paris.

Bonte, P. 1991. *Rapport de Synthèse le Projet Elevage II (Mauritanie) et les Relations Inter-Ethniques*. Paris: Laboratoire d'Anthropologie Sociale.

Boudet, G. and others. 1987. "Pâturages et Elevage au Sud de la Mauritanie (KAEDI); Etude Intégrée sur les Pâturages, Leur Conservation et Leur Restauration, les Cheptel et les Eleveurs." IEMVT, IMRS, CNERV, Maisons Alfort, France.

Boutrais, J. 1985. "Le Développement de l'Elevage dans l'Ouest Centrafricain; Etude Socio-Economique." Ministère de Développement Rural, Bangui.

Bovin, M., 1985. "Nomades Sauvages et Paysan Civilisés; WoDaabe et Kanuri au Bauro" in *Journal des Africanistes*, Musée de l'Homme, Tome 55, Fasc. 1-2, pp 53-74, Paris.

Bovin, M. and L. Manger, eds. 1990. *Adaptive Strategies in African Arid Lands*. Uppsala: The Scandinavian Institute of African Studies.

Bromley, D. W. and M. M. Cernea. 1989. *The Management of Common Property Natural Resources. Some Conceptual and Operational Fallacies*. World Bank Discussion Paper 57. Washington, D.C.

CABO. 1990. "Compétition pour des Ressources Limitées: Le Cas de la Cinquième Région du Mali." Rapport 1-5, Wageningen, Pays-Bas et ESPR, Mopti, Mali.

CARL BRO. 1989. "A Livestock Development Study in the Sahel to Assess the Potential Role of Livestock in Integrated Farming." Draft Report to the World Bank, DANIDA/ World Bank.

Centre Suivi Ecologique. Dakar. Personal Communication. Cernea, M. M. 1989. *User Groups as Producers in Participatory Afforestation Strategies*. World Bank Discussion Paper 70. Washington, D.C.

Cisse, S. 1991. "Working Paper for the Study Team". NORAGRIC-AUN (unpublished).

Conroy, C. and Litvinoff, M. 1988. *The Greening of Aid: Sustainable Livelihood in Practice*. London: Earthscan Publications.

Deniau, P. 1989. *Evaluation Rétrospective du Projet de Développement de l'Elevage au Sénégal Oriental*. Paris: Caisse Centrale de Coopération Economique.

Diakite, N., and M. Keita. 1988. *L'Elevage en 5ème Région: Contraintes et Actions Prioritaires d'Intervention et de Recherche Appliquée*. Bamako, Mali: ODEM (Opération de Développement de l'Elevage dans la Région de Mopti).

Dregne, H. E., 1983. *Desertification of Arid Lands, Advances in Desert and Arid Land Technology and Development*. Chur, Switzerland; New York: Harwood Academic Press.

Dregne, H. E. and C. J. Tucker. 1988. "Desert Encroachment, Desertification Control." Bulletin No. 16, UNEP, Nairobi.

Dupire, M. 1970. *Organisation Sociale des Peul, Etude d'Ethnographie Comparée*. Paris: Plon.

Dupire, M. 1975. "Exploitation du Sol, Communautés Résidentielles et Organisation Lignagère des Pasteurs Wodaabe (Niger)." In *Pastoralism in Tropical Africa*, ed. T. Monod, London: Oxford University Press.

Ellis, J. E., and D. M. Swift. 1988. "Stability of African Pastoral Ecosystems. Alternate Paradigms and Implications for Development." *Journal of Range Management 41(6)*.

Falloux, F., and A. Mukendi, eds. 1987. *Desertification Control and Renewable Resource Management in the Sahelian and Sudanian Zones of West Africa*. World Bank Technical Paper 70, ISBN 082130948. Washington, D.C.

Glantz, M. H., ed, 1977. *Desertification. Environmental Degradation in and around Arid Lands*. Colorado: Westview, Boulder.

Gorse, J. E., and D. R. Steeds. 1987. *Desertification in the Sahelian and Sudanian Zones of West Africa*. World Bank Technical Paper 61. Washington, D.C.

Gorse, J., Y. Gazzo and J. Thomson (consultants). 1988. "Management of Natural Resources in the West African Sahel (with reference to Senegal and Mali): An Assessment." Consultants' Report. World Bank, Africa Technical Department, Agriculture Division, Washington, D.C.

Le Grand, Y. 1988. *Projet pour l'Accélération de l'Emancipation des GIS mise en Place par le PDESO, Etude de Faisabilité*. Dakar: PDESO.

Grainger, A. 1990. *The Threatening Desert: Controlling Desertification*, London: Earthscan Publications.

Gritzner, J. A. 1988. *The West African Sahel: Human Agency and Environmental Change*. Geography Research Paper 226. University of Chicago, Chicago.

Haaland, G., ed. 1982. *Problems of Savannah Development: the Sudan Case*. African Savannah Studies, Occasional Paper 19. Department of Social Anthropology, Bergen.

de Haan, C. 1986. "Constraints and Development Possibilities of Rangeland and Pastoral Systems in Sub-Saharan Africa." Paper presented at the Workshop on "Constraints to Livestock Development and Improvement on Animal Health," Berlin, Germany, January 23-28, 1986.

de Haan, C. 1990a. "Changing Trends in the World Bank's Lending Program for Rangeland Development." Paper to be presented at the International Rangeland Symposium, Reno, February 15, 1990.

de Haan, C. 1990b. "Livestock Development and Bank Lending in Sub-Saharan Africa." Paper presented at an internal World Bank Seminar on the Future of Livestock Lending in Sub-Saharan Africa. World Bank, Washington, D.C.

de Haan, C., and S. Bekure. 1991. *Animal Health Services in Sub-Saharan Africa: Initial Experiences with New Approaches*. World Bank Technical Paper 134. Washington, D.C.

Harrison, P. 1989. *The Greening of Africa, Breaking through the Battle for Land and Food*. London: IIED, Earthscan/ Paladin Grafton Books.

Helland, J. 1984. "Pastoralists and the Development of Pastoralism." Bergen Occasional Papers in Social Anthropology, University of Bergen.

Helldén, U. 1984. *A Remote Sensing Study of Desertification in Kordofan, Sudan*. Sweden: Lund University.

Hjort af Ornas, A., and M. A. M. Sahli, eds, 1989. *Ecology and Politics: Environmental Stress and Security in Africa*. Uppsala: Scandinavian Institute of African Studies.

Horowitz, M. M., and P. D. Little. 1987. *African Pastoralism and Poverty. Some Implications for Drought and Famine: Drought and Hunger in Africa, Denying*

Famine a Future. ed. M. Glantz London: Cambridge University Press.

Le Houérou, H. N. 1977. "Biological Recovery Versus Desertification." *Economic Geography* 53:413-420.

Le Houérou, H. N. 1989. "The Grazing Land Ecosystems of the African Sahel." In *Ecological Studies*, Vol. 75. Springer Verlag.

IRAM. 1991. *Rapport d'Evaluation del'ODEM*. Paris: IRAM.

IUCN. 1989. *The IUCN Sahel Studies 1989: The IUCN Sahel Programme*. Gland, Switzerland.

Kotschi, J. 1986. "Towards Control of Desertification in African Drylands: Problems, Experiences and Guidelines." Sonder Publikation de Deutsche Gesellschaft Fuer Technische Zusammenarbeit, Eschborn, Germany.

Krebs, J., and M. Coe. 1985. "An Ecological Perspective on the Sahel Famine." *Nature* 317:13.

Leng, G. 1982. *Desertification: A Bibliography with Regional Emphasis on Africa*. Universitat Bremen.

Lewis, J. 1989. *Natural Resource Management in the Sahel: An Operational Strategy for Program Development*. Washington, D.C.: World Bank.

Little, P., and M. Horowitz, eds. 1987. *Lands at Risk in the Third World: Local Level Perspectives*. Boulder: Westview.

Mali, Ministère de l'Environnement et de l'Elevage. 1989. *Séminaire National sur les Associations Pastorales et le Développement*. Sujet: "Un Organisme de Développement à la Base: Le Cas de PRODESO." Bamako, Mali.

Marty, A. 1985. "Crise Rurale en Milieu Nord Sahélien et Recherche Coopérative. L'Expérience des Régions de Gao et Tombouctou." Mali 1975-1982, Ph.D thesis, Université François Rabelais, Tours.

Marty, A. 1990. "Les Organisations Coopératives en Milieu Pastoral: Héritage et Enjeux, Sociétés Pastorales et Développement. *Cahiers des Sciences Humaines*, 26(1) and (2), Paris: ORSTOM.

McIntire, J. 1990. "Managing Risk in African Pastoralism," *Tenth Agricultural Symposium*. Washington, D.C.: World Bank.

Msellati, M., and C. Potin. 1990. *Projet National de Développement de l'Elevage, Rapport de la Mission d'Evaluation à Mi-Parcours*. Vol. 1 and Vol. 2 (Annexes), IEMVT, Maisons Alfort, France.

Monod, T., ed. 1975. *Pastoralism in Tropical Africa*. Oxford: OUP.

Moris, J. 1986. "Directions in Contemporary Pastoral Development." Pastoral Development Network Paper 22a, ODI, London.

Nekby, B. A. 1990. "Sub-Saharan Africa. Dryland Management: The Search for Sustainable Development Options." Africa Technical Department, Environment Division, World Bank, Washington, D.C.

Nelson, R. 1988. *Dryland Management: The "Desertification" Problem*. Environment Department Working Paper 8, World Bank, Washington, D.C.

Nelson, R. 1991. "Managing Drylands." *Finance and Development*. March 1991.

Niamir, M., ed, 1990. "Herder's Decision-Making in Natural Resources Management in Arid and Semi-Arid Africa." Community Forestry Note 4, FAO, Rome.

Niamir, M. 1991. "Traditional African Range Management Techniques: Implications for Rangeland Management." ODI Pastoral Development Network Paper 31, London.

Niger, Ministère des Ressources Animales et de l'Hydraulique. 1989. *Projet de Développement de l'Elevage au Niger Centre-Est, Rapport d'Evaluation: Fin 1987 au Mars 1989*. SEDES, Paris.

NORAGRIC. 1990. *IGADD Forum on Environmental Protection and Development of Sub-regional Strategy to Combat Desertification*. Aas, Norway: NORAGRIC - AUN.

ODEM (Opération de Développement de l'Elevage dans la Région de Mopti), Ministère des Ressources Naturelles et de l'Elevage. 1987. "Creation et Formation d'Associations Pastorales à l'ODEM: Strategies et Implications." Document de Reference, Bamako, Mali.

ODEM. 1987. *Les Unités Pastorales: Approche Juridique*. Bamako, Mali.

ODEM. 1989. "Organisations Pastorales et Développement Cas de l'ODEM." *Communication Séminaire National*. Bamako, Mali.

Olsson, L. 1985. *An Integrated Study of Desertification*. Land Studies in Geography No. 13. Sweden: Lund University, Sweden.

Oxby, C. 1978. "Inequality in Pastoral Society and Response to Drought: the Tuareg and the Woodaabe of Niger." Paper of the Conference of Central Bilad Al-Sudan: "Tradition and Adaption," Khartoum, 1977.

Oxby, C. 1985. "Settlement Schemes for Herders in the Sub-humid Tropics of West Africa: Issues of Land Rights and Ethnicity. "ODI Pastoral Development Network Paper No. 19f, February 1985, London.

Oxby, C. 1987. "Women Unveiled: Class and Gender among Kel Ferwan Tuareg (Niger)." In *Ethnos: Swedish Folkens Museum*. Oslo: Scandinavian University Press.

Perrier G.K., 1986. "Limiting Livestock Pressure on Public Rangeland in Niger." ODI Pastoral Development Network, Paper 21d, February 1986, London.

PDESO (Projet de Développement de l'Elevage au Sénégal Oriental). 1986. *Actes du Séminaire Inter-Etats sur les Associations Pastorales*. Tambacounda, Sénégal.

Raynaut, C. 1988. *Le Développement Rural de la Region au Village: Analyser et Comprendre la Diversité*. Bordeaux: GRID, Université de Bordeaux II.

Rigby, P. 1985. *Persistent Pastoralists: Nomadic Societies in Transition*. London: Third World Books, Zed Books Ltd.

RIM. 1987. *Refuge in the Sahel, Livestock Populations and Production Systems in the Mali Fifth Region*. Mopti: ODEM.

Rochette, R. M. 1989. "Lessons of the Fight against the Desertification of the Sahel (Prologue)." Paper presented at Regional Encounter: Local Level Natural Resources Management in the Sahel, Segou, Mali, 22-27 May 1989.

Rochette, R. M., ed. 1989. "Le Sahel en Lutte Contre la Désertification: Leçons d'Expériences." *Programme Allemand CILSS*. Weikersheim, Germany GTZ: Verlag Josef Magraf.

Sandford, S. 1981. "Review of the World Bank Livestock Activities in Dry Tropical Africa." Draft World Bank Document, Washington, D.C.

Sandford, S. 1983. *Management of Pastoral Development in the Third World*. London: John Wiley and Sons and Overseas Development Institute.

Scoones, I., 1988. *Sustainable Pastoralism in Africa, An Annotated Bibliography*. London: IIED Drylands Programme.

Shanmugaratnam, N., S. Moe, S. Rysstad, and P. Vedeld. 1989. *Land Management and Livestock Projects, Botswana; a Review of Environmental Issues*. Report to the World Bank, NORAGRIC, Aas.

Sidibé, A. G. 1989. *Séminaire National sur les Associations et le Développement*. Sujet: "Les Appuis Techniques et Socio-Economiques." Bamako, Mali.

Sihm, P. A., 1989. "Pastoral Associations in West Africa: Experience and Future Strategy." Working paper for Professional Development Workshop on Dryland Management, Africa Technical Department, Agriculture Division, World Bank, Washington, D.C.

Swift, J., ed. 1984. *Pastoral Development in Central Niger: Report of the Niger Range and Livestock Project*. Niamey: Ministère du Développement Rural, Service de l'Elevage.

Swift, J. and A. Maliki. 1984. "A Coopérative Development Experiment among Nomadic Herders in Niger." ODI Pastoral Development Network Paper 18c, September 1984, London.

Swift, J., ed, 1985. *Pastoral and Agropastoral Production Systems in Central Mali: Three Case Studies*. Bamako and Addis Ababa: International Livestock Centre for Africa (ILCA).

Swift, J., C. Toulmin, and S. Chatting. 1988. *Organising Services for Nomadic People: A Review of Literature and Annotated Bibliography*. New York: UNICEF.

Swift, J. 1988. *Major Issues in African Pastoral Development*. Rome: Institute of Development Studies, University of Sussex, FAO.

Swift, J. 1989. "Land Tenure and Pastoral Resource Conservation." In *The IUCN Sahel Studies 1989*. The IUCN Sahel Programme, IUCN.

Sørbø, G. M. 1985. *Tenants and Nomads in Eastern Sudan: A Study of Economic Adaptions in the New Halfa Scheme*. Uppsala: SIAS.

Tacher, G. 1986. *Projet de Développement de l'Elevage dans l'Ouest: Evaluation Ex Post*. Bangui. Talle, A., 1988. *Women at a Loss: Changes in Maasai Pastoralism and their Effects on Gender Relations*. Stockholm.

Thébaud, B. 1986. *L'Eau et les Eleveurs au Sahel: Réflexions sur les Problèmes liés à l'Hydraulique Pastorale en Milieu Sahélien à partir de l'Exemple de l'Est du Niger*.

Thébaud, B., et N. Abdoulaye. 1987. "L'Aménagement de l'Elevage dans le Département de Diffa: Premier Bilan des Principaux Systèmes de Production et Eléments d'Intervention." Projet de Développement de l'Elevage dans le Niger Centre-Est (PDENCE), Niamey.

Thébaud, B. 1988. *Elevage et Développement au Niger: Quel Avenir pour les Eleveurs du Sahel?* Genève: Bureau International du Travail (ILO).

Thébaud, B. 1990. "Politiques d'Hydraulique Pastorale et Gestion de l'Espace au Sahel, Sociétés Pastorales et Développement." *Cahiers des Sciences Humaines 26(1) 1 and (2)*, ORSTOM, Paris.

Toulmin, C. 1983. "Economic Behavior among Livestock-Keeping People: A Review of the Literature on the Economics of Pastoral Production in the Semi-Arid Zones of Africa." Development Studies Occasional Paper 25, School of Development Studies, University of East Anglia, Norwich.

Trolldalen, J. M. and S. W. Bie. 1990."Dryland Management Guidelines: Environment Department." World Bank, Washington, D.C.

UN Economic Commission for Africa. 1985. "Comprehensive Policies and Programmes for Livestock Development in Africa: Problems, Constraints and Necessary Future Action." ALPAN, African Livestock Policy Paper, Network Paper 5, September 1985, Addis Ababa.

UNEP. 1992. *Status of Desertification and Implementation of United Nations Plan of Action to Combat Desertification*. Report of the Executive Director, Governing Council, Nairobi.

UN Sudano-Sahelian Office. 1992. *Assessment of Desertification and Drought in the Sudano-Sahelian Region 1985-1991*. New York: UNSO.

UN Sudano-Sahelian Office. 1990. *Drought and Desertification in the Context of the United Nations Programme of Action for African Economic Recovery and Development (UNPAAERD) 1986-1990*. New York: UNSO.

Van Raay, H. G. T., 1975. *Rural Planning in Savanna Region*. Rotterdam: Rotterdam University Press.

Warren, A. and C. Agnew. 1988. "An Assess ment of Desertification and Land Degradation in Arid and Semi-Arid Areas." IIED Drylands Programme, Issues Envelope, London.

White, C., 1984. *Herd Reconstitution: The Role of Credit among Wodabee Herders in Central Niger*. ODI Pastoral Development Network Paper 18d, London.

Widstrand, C. G. 1975. "The Rationale of Nomad Economy." *Ambio 4(4)*. World Bank. 1985. *The Smallholder Dimension of Livestock Development: A Review of Bank Experience*. Operations Evaluation Department, Division 1, Washington, D.C.

World Bank. 1988. *Rural Development, World Bank Experience, 1965-86*. Operations Evaluation Department, Washington, D.C.

World Bank, 1989. *Sub-Saharan Africa: From Crisis to Sustainable Growth. A Long-Term Perspective Study*. Africa Technical Department, Washington, D.C.

World Bank. 1990. *World Development Report 1990: Poverty*. Report No. 8507, Washington, D.C.

Worley, B. A. 1987. "Property and Gender Relations among Tuareg Nomads." *Nomadic Peoples* 23.

Distributors of World Bank Publications

ARGENTINA
Carlos Hirsch, SRL
Galeria Guemes
Florida 165, 4th Floor-Ofc. 453/465
1333 Buenos Aires

AUSTRALIA, PAPUA NEW GUINEA, FIJI, SOLOMON ISLANDS, VANUATU, AND WESTERN SAMOA
D.A. Books & Journals
648 Whitehorse Road
Mitcham 3132
Victoria

AUSTRIA
Gerold and Co.
Graben 31
A-1011 Wien

BANGLADESH
Micro Industries Development Assistance Society (MIDAS)
House 5, Road 16
Dhanmondi R/Area
Dhaka 1209

Branch offices:
156, Nur Ahmed Sarak
Chittagong 4000

76, K.D.A. Avenue
Kulna 9100

BELGIUM
Jean De Lannoy
Av. du Roi 202
1060 Brussels

CANADA
Le Diffuseur
C.P. 85, 1501B rue Ampère
Boucherville, Québec
J4B 5E6

CHILE
Invertec IGT S.A.
Americo Vespucio Norte 1165
Santiago

CHINA
China Financial & Economic Publishing House
8, Da Fo Si Dong Jie
Beijing

COLOMBIA
Infoenlace Ltda.
Apartado Aereo 34270
Bogota D.E.

COTE D'IVOIRE
Centre d'Edition et de Diffusion Africaines (CEDA)
04 B.P. 541
Abidjan 04 Plateau

CYPRUS
Cyprus College Bookstore
6, Diogenes Street, Engomi
P.O. Box 2006
Nicosia

DENMARK
SamfundsLitteratur
Rosenoerns Allé 11
DK-1970 Frederiksberg C

DOMINICAN REPUBLIC
Editora Taller, C. por A.
Restauración e Isabel la Católica 309
Apartado de Correos 2190 Z-1
Santo Domingo

EGYPT, ARAB REPUBLIC OF
Al Ahram
Al Galaa Street
Cairo

The Middle East Observer
41, Sherif Street
Cairo

FINLAND
Akateeminen Kirjakauppa
P.O. Box 128
SF-00101 Helsinki 10

FRANCE
World Bank Publications
66, avenue d'Iéna
75116 Paris

GERMANY
UNO-Verlag
Poppelsdorfer Allee 55
D-5300 Bonn 1

HONG KONG, MACAO
Asia 2000 Ltd.
46-48 Wyndham Street
Winning Centre
2nd Floor
Central Hong Kong

INDIA
Allied Publishers Private Ltd.
751 Mount Road
Madras - 600 002

Branch offices:
15 J.N. Heredia Marg
Ballard Estate
Bombay - 400 038

13/14 Asaf Ali Road
New Delhi - 110 002

17 Chittaranjan Avenue
Calcutta - 700 072

Jayadeva Hostel Building
5th Main Road Gandhinagar
Bangalore - 560 009

3-5-1129 Kachiguda Cross Road
Hyderabad - 500 027

Prarthana Flats, 2nd Floor
Near Thakore Baug, Navrangpura
Ahmedabad - 380 009

Patiala House
16-A Ashok Marg
Lucknow - 226 001

Central Bazaar Road
60 Bajaj Nagar
Nagpur 440010

INDONESIA
Pt. Indira Limited
Jl. Sam Ratulangi 37
P.O. Box 181
Jakarta Pusat

ISRAEL
Yozmot Literature Ltd.
P.O. Box 56055
Tel Aviv 61560
Israel

ITALY
Licosa Commissionaria Sansoni SPA
Via Duca Di Calabria, 1/1
Casella Postale 552
50125 Firenze

JAPAN
Eastern Book Service
Hongo 3-Chome, Bunkyo-ku 113
Tokyo

KENYA
Africa Book Service (E.A.) Ltd.
Quaran House, Mfangano Street
P.O. Box 45245
Nairobi

KOREA, REPUBLIC OF
Pan Korea Book Corporation
P.O. Box 101, Kwangwhamun
Seoul

MALAYSIA
University of Malaya Cooperative Bookshop, Limited
P.O. Box 1127, Jalan Pantai Baru
59700 Kuala Lumpur

MEXICO
INFOTEC
Apartado Postal 22-860
14060 Tlalpan, Mexico D.F.

NETHERLANDS
De Lindeboom/InOr-Publikaties
P.O. Box 202
7480 AE Haaksbergen

NEW ZEALAND
EBSCO NZ Ltd.
Private Mail Bag 99914
New Market
Auckland

NIGERIA
University Press Limited
Three Crowns Building Jericho
Private Mail Bag 5095
Ibadan

NORWAY
Narvesen Information Center
Book Department
P.O. Box 6125 Etterstad
N-0602 Oslo 6

PAKISTAN
Mirza Book Agency
65, Shahrah-e-Quaid-e-Azam
P.O. Box No. 729
Lahore 54000

PERU
Editorial Desarrollo SA
Apartado 3824
Lima 1

PHILIPPINES
International Book Center
Fifth Floor, Filipinas Life Building
Ayala Avenue, Makati
Metro Manila

POLAND
International Publishing Service
Ul. Piekna 31/37
00-677 Warzawa

For subscription orders:
IPS Journals
Ul. Okrezna 3
02-916 Warszawa

PORTUGAL
Livraria Portugal
Rua Do Carmo 70-74
1200 Lisbon

SAUDI ARABIA, QATAR
Jarir Book Store
P.O. Box 3196
Riyadh 11471

SINGAPORE, TAIWAN, MYANMAR, BRUNEI
Information Publications Private, Ltd.
Golden Wheel Building
41, Kallang Pudding, #04-03
Singapore 1334

SOUTH AFRICA, BOTSWANA
For single titles:
Oxford University Press Southern Africa
P.O. Box 1141
Cape Town 8000

For subscription orders:
International Subscription Service
P.O. Box 41095
Craighall
Johannesburg 2024

SPAIN
Mundi-Prensa Libros, S.A.
Castello 37
28001 Madrid

Librería Internacional AEDOS
Consell de Cent, 391
08009 Barcelona

SRI LANKA AND THE MALDIVES
Lake House Bookshop
P.O. Box 244
100, Sir Chittampalam A. Gardiner Mawatha
Colombo 2

SWEDEN
For single titles:
Fritzes Fackboksforetaget
Regeringsgatan 12, Box 16356
S-103 27 Stockholm

For subscription orders:
Wennergren-Williams AB
Box 30004
S-104 25 Stockholm

SWITZERLAND
For single titles:
Librairie Payot
1, rue de Bourg
CH 1002 Lausanne

For subscription orders:
Librairie Payot
Service des Abonnements
Case postale 3312
CH 1002 Lausanne

TANZANIA
Oxford University Press
P.O. Box 5299
Maktaba Road
Dar es Salaam

THAILAND
Central Department Store
306 Silom Road
Bangkok

TRINIDAD & TOBAGO, ANTIGUA BARBUDA, BARBADOS, DOMINICA, GRENADA, GUYANA, JAMAICA, MONTSERRAT, ST. KITTS & NEVIS, ST. LUCIA, ST. VINCENT & GRENADINES
Systematics Studies Unit
#9 Watts Street
Curepe
Trinidad, West Indies

TURKEY
Infotel
Narlabahçe Sok. No. 15
Cagaloglu
Istanbul

UNITED KINGDOM
Microinfo Ltd.
P.O. Box 3
Alton, Hampshire GU34 2PG
England

VENEZUELA
Libreria del Este
Aptdo. 60.337
Caracas 1060-A